The Spokesman

The War on Terror Runs Amok

Edited by Ken Coates

**Published by Spokesman for the
Bertrand Russell Peace Foundation**

Spokesman 75   **2002**

CONTENTS

Subscriptions
Institutions £30.00
Individuals £20.00 (UK)
£25.00 (ex UK)

Back issues available on request

A CIP catalogue record for this book is available from the British Library

Published by the
Bertrand Russell Peace Foundation Ltd.,
Russell House
Bulwell Lane
Nottingham NG6 0BT
England
Tel. 0115 9784504
email:
elfeuro@compuserve.com
www.spokesmanbooks.com
www.russfound.org

Printed by the Russell Press Ltd., Nottingham, UK

ISSN 0262 7922   ISBN 0 85124 669 9

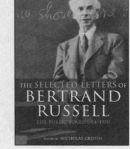

Editorial: Full Spectrum Overreach

In May 2002 the headlines are full of the new relationship between Nato and Russia. This had been coming along quite promisingly, even before the attacks of September 11ᵗʰ. Did not President Bush himself inform the press after the Ljubljana meeting that he had looked Putin in the eye, and contrived thereby 'to get a sense of his soul'. Mr. Putin has not put on record any discoveries he may have made about the soul of George Bush. But wise voices have been heard in Russia, wondering whether over-cordial personal relations between consenting statesmen may cloud their dispassionate judgement.

Meantime, the new relationship is to be institutionalised with the formation of a Nato-Russian Council, widely proclaimed as the final end of the Cold War. We seem to be fated to end the Cold War at recurrent intervals. So the latest 'ending' might not be the last.

But it seems clear that a serious effort is underway to explore the possibilities of a new relationship between the United States and Russia, solidifying an accord on Eurasian security, whilst opening a number of doors to economic 'co-operation'. How co-operative this might prove in reality will evidently influence the durability of the entire relationship. But if the Nato-Russian Council cannot be taken for granted, neither can Nato itself. The events of September 11ᵗʰ are putting some real stresses on the old Alliance.

In the shock of sympathy for the victims of the destruction of the Twin Towers, public opinion in Europe ran very warmly towards the Americans. Nato solemnly resolved to invoke Article Five of the Treaty deeming the events of the September 11ᵗʰ attack on the United States to be an attack on the Alliance as a whole. So activated, the Alliance awaited the call to action. But the United States proved quite unready to involve the institutions of Nato in its war of reprisal against Al Qaeda and the Taliban, or even in its wider war on terrorism. Lessons had been learnt from Yugoslavia, where it had not been unknown for lesser allies to obstruct the will of the principal partner. The Alliance found itself all but stood down: 'Don't call us, we'll call you' being the dominant message. Some individual calls were sent. Indeed, some were not received with enthusiasm. A careful analysis of the behaviour of the Alliance in the face of this emergency is likely to reveal stresses which may come to seem as important as the new accord with Mr. Putin.

All the while, the American war has been widening. President Putin has endorsed a conflict which sees the arc of terror stretching all the way from Chechnya or Georgia, around to the Philippine Islands. American troops are already engaged in Georgia, and in the Philippines (660 of them) and American bases are dotted around at many points in between. Thirteen locations in nine countries near to Afghanistan have mushroomed within the last year. Sixty thousand American personnel are deployed within them. What the Chinese think of the new deployments in Kyrgyzstan, Uzbekistan and Tajikistan, and the others foreseen in Azerbaijan and Kazakhstan is not on the record, but it is not difficult to imagine their response.

The horrific repression in Palestine is also multiplying tensions all across the Middle East, and bringing the American bases there into the eye of controversy. And all this is set within a fearful context of George Bush's war on the axis of evil, nominating old American adversaries as prime candidates for the next round of the war against terror. The projected war against Iraq is opposed by almost every state within the region, and threatens some of the long-term allies of the United States quite directly. A war on Iraq would destabilise Iran, and very possibly spread there.

True, Nato had conveniently redefined its scope, at the Jubilee meeting in Washington in 1999. But in those far off days, 'out of area' might be taken to mean Kosovo or Serbia. Now, Afghanistan, Iraq, Iran are already squarely in the centre of the new area. And North Korea? Cuba? Wherever next?

It is doubtful whether Nato can survive so drastic an enlargement of its appetites. In truth, the appetite in question is that of the dominant right wing of the Republican Party in the United States, and it is shared by very few others in the rest of the world.

In the past, a major reason for the Americans to maintain the Alliance was the maintenance of their influence over the European partners. Will this influence survive the melt-down that is impending? Wars promised, wars threatened, and wars in prospect, will profoundly disturb the pattern of interests which aligned the members of the Alliance into a block. The defection of Putin from the role of first public enemy will remove more of the cement of the Alliance.

How far must the price of petrol rise before Europe discovers a radical divergence of interests from the erstwhile American protector?

Ken Coates

The War on Terror Runs Amok

An Appeal from United States Citizens to Friends in Europe

Following the events of September 11, 2001, a broadside appeal signed by 58 American intellectuals beseeched support for the United States 'war on terrorism'. Subsequently, more than twice that number of writers, academics and other concerned citizens of the United States issued this appeal to friends in Europe to join efforts in stopping President Bush's 'mad rush to war'. The Russell Foundation has circulated this appeal widely. It is reproduced here, together with a selection of the responses we have received so far.

The central fallacy of the pro-war celebrants is the equation between 'American values' as understood at home and the exercise of United States economic and especially military power abroad.

Following the 11 September 2001 suicide attacks on the World Trade Centre in New York and the Pentagon in Washington, US President George W. Bush has declared an open-ended 'war on terrorism'. This war has no apparent limits, in place, time or the extent of destruction that may be inflicted. There is no telling which country may be suspected of hiding 'terrorists' or declared to be part of an 'axis of evil'. The eradication of 'evil' could last much longer than the world can withstand the destructive force to be employed. The Pentagon is already launching bombs described as producing the effect of earthquakes and is officially considering the use of nuclear weapons, among other horrors in its constantly improved arsenal.

The material destruction envisaged is immeasurable. So is the human damage, not only in terms of lives, but also in terms of the moral desperation and hatred that are certain to be felt by millions of people who can only watch helplessly as their world is devastated by a country, the United States, which assumes that its moral authority is as absolute and unchallengeable as its military power.

We, as United States citizens, have a special responsibility to oppose this mad rush to war. You, as Europeans, also have a special responsibility. Most of your countries are military allies of the United States within NATO. The United States claims to act in self-defence, but also to defend 'the interests of its allies and friends'. Your countries will inevitably be implicated in US military adventures. Your future is also in jeopardy.

Many informed people both within and outside your governments are aware of the dangerous folly of the war path followed by the Bush administration. But few dare speak out honestly. They are intimidated by the various forms of retaliation that can be taken against 'friends' and 'allies' who fail to provide unquestioning support. They are afraid of being labelled 'anti-American' – the same label absurdly applied to Americans themselves who speak out against war policies and whose protests are easily drowned out in the chorus of chauvinism dominating the United States media. A sane and frank European criticism of the Bush administration's war policy can help anti-war Americans make their voices heard.

Celebrating power may be the world's oldest profession among poets and men of letters. As supreme world power, the United States naturally attracts its celebrants who urge the nation's political leaders to go ever farther in using their military might to impose virtue on a recalcitrant world. The theme is age-old and forever the same: the goodness of the powerful should be extended to the powerless by the use of force.

The central fallacy of the pro-war celebrants is the equation between 'American values' as understood at home and the exercise of United States economic and especially military power abroad. Self-celebration is a notorious feature of United States culture, perhaps as a useful means of assimilation in an immigrant society. Unfortunately, September 11 has driven this tendency to new extremes. Its effect is to reinforce a widespread illusion among United States citizens that the whole world is fixated, in admiration or in envy, on the United States as it sees itself: prosperous, democratic, generous, welcoming, open to all races and religions, the epitome of universal human values and the last best hope of mankind.

In this ideological context, the question raised after September 11, 'Why do they hate us?' has only one answer: 'Because we are so good!' Or, as is commonly claimed, they hate us because of 'our values'.

Most United States citizens are unaware that the effect of US power abroad has nothing to do with the 'values' celebrated at home, and indeed often serves to deprive people in other countries of the opportunity to attempt to enjoy them should they care to do so.

In Latin America, Africa and Asia, US power has more often than not been used to prop up the remnants of colonial regimes and unpopular dictators, to impose devastating commercial and financial conditions, to support repressive armed forces, to overthrow or cripple by sanctions relatively independent governments, and finally to send bombers and cruise missiles to rain down death and destruction.

The 'Right of Self-Defence'

Whose right? Since September 11, the United States feels under attack. As a result its government claims a 'right to self-defence' enabling it to wage war on its own terms, as it chooses, against any country it designates as an enemy, without proof of guilt or legal procedure.

Obviously, such a 'right of self-defence' never existed for countries such as Vietnam, Laos, Cambodia, Libya, Sudan or Yugoslavia when they were bombed by the United States. Nor will it be recognized for countries bombed by the

United States in the future. This is simply the right of the strongest, the law of the jungle. Exercising such a 'right', denied all others, cannot serve 'universal values' but only undermines the very concept of a world order based on universal values with legal recourse open to all on a basis of equality.

A 'right' enjoyed only by one entity – the most powerful – is not a right but a privilege exercised only to the detriment of the rights of others.

How is the United States to 'defend' itself? Supposedly in self-defence, the United States launched a war against Afghanistan. This was not an action specially designed to respond to the unique events of September 11. On the contrary, it was exactly what the United States was already doing, and had already planned to do, as outlined in Pentagon documents: bomb other countries, send military forces onto foreign soil and topple their governments. The United States is openly planning an all-out war – not excluding use of nuclear weapons – against Iraq, a country it has been bombing for a decade, with the proclaimed aim of replacing its government with leaders selected by Washington.

Precisely what is being 'defended'? What is being defended is related to what was attacked.

Traditionally, 'defence' means defence of national territory. On September 11, an attack actually took place on and against United States territory. This was not a conventional attack by a major power designed to seize territory. Rather, it was an anonymous strike against particular targeted institutions. In the absence of any claim of responsibility, the symbolic nature of the targets may have been assumed to be self-explanatory. The World Trade Centre clearly symbolised United States global economic power, while the Pentagon represented United States military power. Thus, it seems highly unlikely that the September 11 attacks were symbolically directed against 'American values' as celebrated in the United States.

Rather, the true target seems to have been United States economic and military power as it is projected abroad. According to reports, 15 of the 19 identified hijackers were Saudi Arabians hostile to the presence of US military bases on Saudi soil. September 11 suggests that the nation projecting its power abroad is vulnerable at home, but the real issue is United States intervention abroad. Indeed the Bush wars are designed precisely to defend and strengthen United States power abroad. It is US global power projection that is being defended, not domestic freedoms and way of life.

In reality, foreign wars are more likely to undermine the domestic values cherished by civilians at home than to defend or spread them. But governments that wage aggressive wars always drum up domestic support by convincing ordinary people that war is necessary to defend or to spread noble ideas. The principal difference between the imperial wars of the past and the global thrust of the United States today is the far greater means of destruction available. The disproportion between the material power of destruction and the constructive power of human wisdom has never been more dangerously unbalanced. Intellectuals today have the choice of joining the chorus of those who celebrate brute force by rhetorically attaching it to 'spiritual values', or taking up the more difficult and essential task of exposing the arrogant folly of power and working with the whole of humanity to create means of reasonable dialogue, fair economic relations and equal justice.

The right to self-defence must be a collective human right. Humanity as a whole has the right to defend its own survival against the 'self-defence' of an unchecked superpower. For half a century, the United States has repeatedly demonstrated its indifference to the collateral death and destruction wrought by its self-proclaimed efforts to improve the world. Only by joining in solidarity with the victims of US military power can we in the rich countries defend whatever universal values we claim to cherish.

The initial signatories to this appeal include:

Norman Birnbaum, Professor Emeritus, Georgetown University Law Centre

Helen Caldicott, paediatrician, author, founder of Physicians for Social Responsibility

Edward S. Herman, economist and media analyst, Philadelphia

Diana Johnstone, journalist, Paris

Harry Magdoff, co-editor, *Monthly Review*, New York City

James Petras, State University of New York, Binghamton

Paul M. Sweezy, co-editor, *Monthly Review*, New York City

Gore Vidal, writer, Los Angeles

Howard Zinn, writer, Boston, Massachusetts

A full list appears on page 15.

*   *   *   *

When the Russell Foundation received this Appeal, we circulated it throughout the European Network for Peace and Human Rights, and among a number of longstanding contributors to The Spokesman. We think that the responses we have received are interesting, and here we feature some of them.

From the journalist Felicity Arbuthnot

Mesapotamia – 'Axis of evil'

Luay was ten years old when he found the head, during the Gulf War. He told his story to Professor Magne Raundalen, founder of the Centre for Crisis Studies, in Bergen, Norway and one of the world's foremost experts on the trauma of children in war.

Luay had joined a 'neighbourhood watch' scheme – groups who tried to rescue people from bombed buildings. Since he was small, he could reach places that others couldn't. Crawling into one building, he told Raundalen, he had found the body of 'a mother'. Crawling further on, he found the body of her baby. He described how he had crawled back through the rubble and placed the baby on the mother's breast and wrapped her still warm arms round him. 'That is your worst memory?' asked Raundalen; no his 'worst memory was the head'.

Crawling back, he had found a jacket, and under it was a head. He dreamed every night that he was taking the head from his jacket pocket and handing it to the rescuers to try and identify it for a bereaved family and a dignified burial.

In surveys, Raundelen found that up to eighty per cent of children felt they would not live to grow up and he found, in Iraq, 'the most traumatised child population' he had ever encountered.

Luay will now be twenty-two – if he has not become one of the up to eleven thousand a month who die of 'embargo related causes'. Five to six thousand of those are under five. If he has survived the grinding misery of the most draconian siege ever administered by the United Nations, he will now be conscripted into Iraq's decimated army and probably end his lost youth as cannon fodder for a smart or truly dumb missile.

On one visit to Iraq, I asked young people, at random, from all backgrounds, of their hopes dreams and fears. None had a dream. 'I am too tired to dream', said an eighteen year old who had once dreamed of being a doctor. He was working in a smelter, to support his family, in the searing heat of Baghdad, as it paid pitifully, but relatively well in a land where a kilo of meat – due to stratospheric inflation – at that time, exceeded a university professor's monthly salary. A young woman dreamed 'of having enough milk for my baby'. Another waited till her mother left the room and whispered: 'nothing awaits us, only death.' She was eighteen.

Forgotten, too, are the numerous bombings by Britain and the United States – unsanctioned by the United Nations and the trauma they continue to heap on this shattered, damaged youth, in the land where Abraham was born at Ur, which brought the world writing, mathematics, algebra, record keeping, and the first domestic laws were written before the birth of Christ. Where the Garden of Eden flourished, and the site of the hanging gardens of Babylon can still be visited.

A friend, who arranged for all the neighbourhood children to come to his house when there was a bombing, in peer support, hesitated, before saying: 'I hope you won't be offended, when I tell you that, when the bombing stops, we are left, in the dark, surrounded by pools of urine and faeces, from the terror of the children.' In Orwell-speak of the Ministry of Defence and the Pentagon, like Luay's head: 'collateral damage'.

In February 1998, when the world was certain Iraq was going to be bombed again, I was in Baghdad and went to visit a woman with another tragic tale to tell. Like many, she had sold all her furniture to survive. As we talked in her large, bare room, it began to fill with children – a stranger in this isolated land is a rare treat. They sat, perhaps fifty in all, aged between perhaps three and thirteen, quiet as mice, watching every move of my pen.

When I got up to leave, dusk was falling and they followed me out and as I got into the battered car, they surrounded it, laughing, waving and blowing kisses. As we moved off, they ran beside us, still laughing, smiling and blowing kisses. When we were moving too fast I looked back and they were standing in a knot in the road, still, laughing and blowing kisses. It was the darkest night, the night all the military experts said Iraq would be bombed again. I went back to my hotel, lay on the bed and wept.

Public opinion prevented the February bombing. Instead, in December Prime Minister Blair stood in front of his resplendent Christmas tree and announced we were bombing (in time for Christmas and Ramadan.)

If this illegal, immoral, tragi-ridiculous 'war on terrorism' continues, not alone the Middle East, but most of the world will erupt; we are truly looking into the abyss. That 'history will slaughter those responsible' to quote distinguished former UN Under Secretary General, Denis Halliday, will be of no comfort to the traumatised children of Iraq, Palestine, Afghanistan and wherever else this feckless, reckless policy leads.

From Tony Benn

The statement issued by American intellectuals should be widely welcomed as a confirmation of what most thoughtful people in the world know to be true, namely that the policies of the United States administration do not represent the view of many millions of Americans. Links between us across the Atlantic and across the world are essential if we are to build a mass popular movement – as we must – for Peace and Social Justice.

From John Berger

I endorse this statement wholeheartedly and I salute the lucidity and courage of its authors.

From Peter Cadogan, London Alliance

As I write this I am aware that the big demonstration at the White House is at this moment building up for its 1pm start. That build-up has been going on for months. This could be a critical day. The action is organised by an ad hoc association – ANSWER – bringing all sorts together to get maximum impact.

The whole world is at threat as never before – this time from US military and financial arrogance without precedent. There is no way our traditional peace movement can cope with this. Effective resistance has already begun in at least five quarters. They are (in no particular order):

First, from the American people themselves – witness today's demonstration. And this includes from within the United States Government where, notoriously, different Departments pursue different and even contrary policies.

Second, the European Union – which has yet to get its act together over foreign policy and defence, but where a first line of resistance is already apparent in the demand that all United States action shall be first cleared by the United Nations Security Council. This could be good.

Third, resistance from the indigenous peoples of the world, led by those of Latin America – in Mexico, Argentina, Brazil, Venezuela and elsewhere.

Fourth, the special case of involvement of Arab peoples and Muslims more widely, arising out of the immediate concentration of US indirect attack on

Palestine (via Sharon) and the continued intention to invade Iraq. This attack, it seems, has been put back for at least twelve months and even longer. Saudi Arabia has already started to put its foot down and the United States has been obliged to move its main military base from Saudi Arabia to Qatar.

Fifth, resistance from our kind of peace and human rights movement throughout the world.

There are doubtless dozens of other elements involved. This is only a start in their analysis. Is there a pecking order? Is there a cutting edge? My hunch is that the ultimate key to resistance has to be in the United States. If that is the case the vital matter is that everyone lines up in its support, starting from today. But we have to watch points daily and rethink as need be. This could be the big one.

From Liz Davies, Chairperson, Socialist Alliance

The attitude of the United States and British governments towards the murderous policies of the Israeli state has thrown into sharp relief the hypocrisy of their self-proclaimed 'war on terrorism'. The United States government invoked the right of nations to self-defence in support of its attack on Afghanistan. Yet, when the Palestinians are attacked and murdered and when Arafat is held prisoner in his own office, the United States and British governments refuse to condemn Israel's actions, and continue to sell arms to Israel. Without the support of the United States and British governments, Israel would be internationally isolated and unable to continue its assault on the Palestinians.

The so-called 'war on terrorism' was a convenient opportunity for the United States, British and other governments. Civil liberties in the States, Britain, India and elsewhere have been restricted. In Britain, New Labour was only too delighted to use 11 September as a pretext to introduce arbitrary detention of foreign nationals – a measure specifically prohibited by the European Convention of Human Rights which Britain signs up to.

The peace movement in Europe has grown extensively since 11 September. In Britain, public opinion is opposed to an invasion of Iraq – over 100,000 people demonstrated against the war in Afghanistan last November. There have been anti-war demonstrations in all the major European cities. At first, those of us opposed to the war in Afghanistan were accused of being 'anti-American'. We are not anti-American; however, we are opposed to American foreign policy and in particular to the United States government's attempt to police the world in the interests of the rich and powerful of the West, and in the interests of globalisation.

From Carol Fox, co-founder of the Peace and Neutrality Alliance;
co-founder of US Citizens in Ireland for Alternatives to War

'A Letter from United States Citizens to Friends in Europe' is to be strongly welcomed and supported. This appeal gives the lie to the claim that Americans are fully backing President Bush in his Crusade against terrorism and global evil. I am writing as a US Citizen who has lived for nearly thirty years in Ireland, so

I identify very much with the Appeal's statement that both Europeans and US citizens have a 'special responsibility to oppose this mad rush to war'. The Bertrand Russell Peace Foundation is to be thanked for providing this forum.

There are no borders or limits set to the War Against Terrorism. The Bush Administration has taken the gloves off in terms of the types of weapons it's willing to deploy (nuclear included) and in terms of obeying the rules of the game. The Bush Rule Book has constructed a lawless model of international behaviour which has already bred chaos and bloodshed and given licence to such horrors as the Israelis' levelling of Palestinian towns to Ground Zero scenes of rubble, death and destruction.

As firm friends of the United States, Ireland is one of those countries (as the appeal puts it) 'implicated in US military adventures'. Ireland is more than implicated. Although still technically a neutral country and not in NATO, Ireland has provided airport facilities at Shannon Airport and transit rights to United States warplanes and soldiers in the war against Afghanistan, and given full diplomatic backing to the War Against Terrorism. The anti-war movement in Ireland – including a group called 'U.S. Citizens in Ireland for Alternatives to War' – has highlighted these issues and opinion polls show a majority of Irish people are opposed to Shannon Airport being used in the war effort. There is no doubt that opposition will continue to grow and that the Irish Government and other European Union States will have to respond to a public opinion that will not support an open-ended US war effort. US Citizens speaking out on this issue, and appealing to Europeans for backing, helps immensely to counter the charges of anti-Americanism.

From Pierre Galand, Forum Nord-Sud, Belgium

No, I am not anti-american, nor anti-semitic, and I admire all those who, in Israel and in the United States, raise their voices to announce their objections to and their fears about the bellicose and domineering attitudes of the Bush and Sharon governments.

These people, intellectuals and peace activists, are the resistance who safeguard human dignity and make us want to share with them the fight to protect our common heritage : humanity.

'We live in a period full of twilight', said a biologist friend recently. But I am convinced that another world is possible. We will build it together.

From Johan Galtung, Transcend

There seem to be three discourses, competing for attention, to accommodate September 11 (terrorism in New York/Washington, killing about 3,000) and October 7 2001 (state terrorism in Afghanistan, killing about 5,000).

The first is the terrorist discourse. Dominated by fundamentalist Islam and the *shahadah* ('I testify that there is no God but Allah, and I testify that Muhammad is his prophet') and by the sword; the flag of Saudi Arabia is the perfect symbol. Bringing Allah's justice to America is one element. Another, emphasised by bin Laden, is revenge for humiliation: 'What America is tasting now is something insignificant compared to what we have tasted for scores of years. Our nation has been tasting this humiliation and this degradation for more than 80 years'.

The second is the state terrorist discourse, most clearly articulated by fundamentalist USA. In the words of W. J. Bennett, on behalf of Americans for Victory over Terrorism: 'We are a target not because of anything we have done, but because of who we are, what we stand for, what we believe, and what our nation was founded upon: the twin principles of liberty and equality'. Charles Krauthammer in the *Washington Post*: 'America won the Cold War, pocketed Poland and Hungary and the Czech Republic as door prizes, pulverized Serbia and Afghanistan and – highlighted Europe's irrelevance with a display of vast military superiority'. Behind this geo-fascism one can sense Zbigniew Brzezinski's *The Grand Chess-Board: America's Primacy and its Geostrategic Imperatives*. And underlying that, in turn, one senses 'a nation under God'.

Acquaintance with these discourses is indispensable to understand the mental frameworks within which the motivations – and capabilities! – emerge. As pointed out in the opening of the manifesto by 120+ American intellectuals, 'The central fallacy of the pro-war celebrants is the equation between "American values" as understood at home and the exercise of United States economic and especially military power abroad.'

And this is where the third discourse takes off. That discourse will include diagnosis of why 11 September and 7 October happened as parts of a retaliation cycle, but also to use that revenge for other purposes. It would include prognosis of what will happen, such as rejection of fundamentalism on both sides, and of United States policy, not because of overreach relative to military capability, but because of too high military capability. And it would include suggestions for therapy, for instance culturally as dialogue between moderates on all sides; economically by playing down the axis of evil to most people in the world, which is the World Bank-International Monetary Fund-World Trade Organisation triad, as *Le Monde Diplomatique* puts it; diplomatically through conflict resolution in the Middle-East/West Asia; and militarily through United States defence of homeland security, at home.

Washington and Islamic fundamentalists today suffer rapidly growing opposition, governmental and non-governmental, in the West and in the Islamic world. When these forces find each other things will change. (For continuation see www.transcend.org)

From the playwright Trevor Griffiths

Thank you for the statement by American intellectuals on the War on Peace. Let me say at once I endorse both the arguments made and the conclusions drawn in the American document, which I find very inspiring. Rather than pen a few paragraphs of general support, I propose sending you a ten-minute play called *Camel Station*, which I wrote last Fall (see page 16). It was given – along with other pieces by Pinter, Tariq Ali et al – a public reading at the Cooper Hall, New York City before an audience of more than a thousand.

From Caroline Lucas MEP

At this time of increasing global insecurity it is ever more urgent that we stand up to plans for a National Missile Defence programme which is being hatched on both sides of the Atlantic. There's nothing *defensive* about this programme – it is a deeply *offensive* weapons system, specifically designed to bring about fear and instability, which will trigger a major new arms race. It is the military wing of the globalisation project, driven by corporate interests and concerns, to maintain their global control.

True security doesn't lie in National Missile Defence systems, or ever greater military hardware, or ever increasing defence budgets. We will only be more secure when poverty and injustice are eradicated. Until we understand the violence of our economic policies, our military policies, and our foreign policies, we will continue to foster the conditions that make terrorism possible.

Martin Luther King said: 'A time has come when silence is betrayal. That time is now.' Only if we stand up and speak out will we make a difference.

I was very inspired by the letter from the US citizens. Only if we work together globally will we defeat the increasing militarisation which is threatening people and planet.

from Dr A. Sivanandan Director,
Institute of Race Relations; Editor, Race & Class

The world is in danger from America – economically, politically and, now, militarily. Globalisation has engendered a monolithic economic system governed by American corporations that hold nation states in thrall. September 11 has engendered a monolithic political culture that holds that those who are not pro-American are either terrorists or value-less and, therefore, surplus to civilisation. Together, they signal the end of civil society and the beginnings of a new imperialism, brutal and unashamed.

On a more philosophical level, one would have expected that the suffering inflicted on the American people on September 11 would have sensitised them to the suffering of the poor and the deprived of the world. But, alas, they have had the experience and missed the meaning. Worse, they have denied all meaning to their own suffering by inflicting it on others.

We are connected to one another, in the deepest sense, through our common pain. When we lose that connection we lose our humanity.

from Rae Street, former Vice Chair, Campaign for Nuclear Disarmament

It is heartening to read this statement from the 120 – and we know there are thousands more who share the view across the United States. These are the United States friends with whom we stand 'shoulder to shoulder'; those who are opposing the new world order as interpreted by the Bush 'corporate' government. We certainly support all their outspoken criticism of those forces in the United States (often supported by the United Kingdom) which are bringing increasing global instability, and will provoke further acts of terrorism such as were seen on

September 11th.

The anything-is-justified foreign policy has now led to the unabashed statement that the United States government is prepared to use nuclear weapons – provoking terror and similar assertions by other aggressive leaders from Pakistan to (almost unbelievably) Japan. Let us hope that the statement of our friends in the United States is widely read across Europe, from Ireland to Russia.

Initial signatories to the United States Appeal were:

Daphne Abeel, Julie L. Abraham, Michael Albert, Janet Kestenberg Amighi, Electa Arenal, Anthony Arnove, Stanley Aronowitz, Dean Baker, Houston A. Baker, Jr., David Barsamian, Rosalyn Baxandall, Medea Benjamin, Dick Bennett, Larry Bensky, Norman Birnbaum, Joel Bleifuss, Chana Bloch, William Blum, Magda Bogin, Patrick Bond, Charles P. Boyer, Francis A. Boyle, Gray Brechin, Renate Bridenthal, Linda Bullard, Judith Butler, Bob Buzzanco, Helen Caldicott, John Cammett, Stephanie M.H. Camp, Ward Churchill, John P. Clark, Dan Coughlin, Sandi Cooper, Lawrence Davidson, David Devine, Douglas Dowd, Madhu Dubey, Richard B. Du Boff, Peter Erlinder, Francis Feeley, Richard Flynn, Michael S. Foley, John Bellamy Foster, H. Bruce Franklin, Jane Franklin, Oscar H. Gandy, Jr., Jamshed Ghandhi, Larry Gross, Beau Grosscup, Zalmay Gulzad, Thomas J. Gumbleton, Marilyn Hacker, Robin Hahnel, Edward S. Herman, Marc W. Herold, John L. Hess, David U. Himmelstein, W.G. Huff, Adrian Prentice Hull, Marsha Hurst, David Isles, Robert Jensen, Diana Johnstone, John Jonik, Louis Kampf, Mary Kaye, Douglas Kellner, Michael King, Gabriel Kolko, Joyce Kolko, Claudia Koonz, Joel Kovel, Marilyn Krysl, Mark Lance, Ann J. Lane, Karen Latuchie, Peggy Law, Amy Schrager Lang, Helena Lewis, Dave Lindorff, Eric Lott, Angus Love, David MacMichael, Harry Magdoff, Sanjoy Mahajan, Michael Marcus, Robert McChesney, Jo Ann McNamara, Arthur Mitzman, Margaret E. Montoya, Robert Naiman, Marilyn Nelson, Suzanne Oboler, Bertell Ollman, Alicia Ostriker, Christian Parenti, Michael Parenti, Mark Pavlick, Michael Perelman, Jeff Perlstein, David Peterson, James Petras, Joan Pinkham, Lawrence Pinkham, Cathie Platt, Gordon Poole, Douglas Porpora, Larry Portis, Ellen Ray, Elton Rayack, Lillian S. Robinson, Rick Rozoff, Albert Ruben, Sten Rudstrom, William H. Schaap, Ellen Schrecker, Gretchen Seifert, Anne Shaver, Gerald E. Shenk, Mary Shepard, Francis Shor, Robert M. Smith, Alan Sokal, Norman Solomon, William S. Solomon, Sarah Standefer, Abraham Sussman, Malcolm Sylvers, Paul M. Sweezy, Holly Thau, Reetika Vazirani, Gore Vidal, Joe Volk, Lynne Walker, Karin Wilkins, Howard Winant, Steffie Woolhandler, George Wright, Howard Zinn

Camel Station

Trevor Griffiths

Northern No-Fly Zone, Iraq. Mountain pastures near Ninevah. Hot. A small battery radio, on its last legs, relays ecstatic commentary on the Iraq-Iran world cup qualifying match from the national stadium. TARIK, 13, perched on a rock beside it, works on something in a notebook, voicing words and phrases as he writes. He wears traditional arab work-dress, though the kuffiah is round his neck, to make room for the NYY baseball cap shading his eyes. Across his back, an ancient Lee Enfield from the second world war.

> TARIK
> '...The sign read: (thinks) alHourani – Camel Station. Is it a mirage, the tricks of the desert, the Man from Tikrit asked himself. How can this be real?

He looks up at the sky, listens. The radio sputters to nothing. He listens on. A thin wisp of sound from the stratosphere slowly asserts in the silence. He unslings the rifle. Takes aim at the pale blue sky.

> TARIK
> (Sighting) How. Can this. Be. Real?
> (Fakes firing) Boosh. Boosh. Boosh.

A girl's shout from below. Sheep bleat, men call. He looks down the hill, reslings the rifle, returns to his notebook.

> SURIYA
> (Still toiling up) Hey! HeadinaBook. I brought you food. (She arrives, stops by the rock, lays down a muslin-wrapped parcel and a plastic bottle of water.) Surprised to see me? By, you've grown. You're as tall as me. (She fondles his head, he resists) My little cousin. (She drinks from the bottle, hands it to him) They told me down there you were on wolf watch, your father's so rich he can afford to lose his flock..?

Trevor Griffiths's plays include modern classics such as 'The Comedians' and 'The Party'. His television work includes a celebrated version of D.H.Lawrence's 'Sons and Lovers', the screenplay of which is published by Spokesman Books.

She's already looking up. The dull remote groan of a plane reasserts. Tarik sneaks a shy look at her. Black robe, white scarf. Sixteen.

TARIK

My mam said you were in Baghdad. (She scans on) Studying medicine. (Nothing) Too hard, was it?

SURIYA

(Eyes on sky) My mother's sick. I'm looking after her. (The sky) There's nothing there...

TARIK

Reconnaissance. (She looks at him) No pilot. (Returns to his pad) American.

SURIYA

How do you know that?

TARIK

It's Tuesday. Tuesday's America Day. (Turns pages; rubs out a word, writes in another) It'll be sending back your picture. Couple of minutes they'll be here in person. (Shy peek) Taking a look. (He imitates a fighter plane buzzing the hillside, head and mouth) Zooooosh. (Points behind him up the mountain) And if you look up there ... you should be able to make out ...

SURIYA

... Eat, child. Go on. (He fiddles with a piece of cheese) Do you want the fig? (He shrugs, she takes it) Should be able to make out ...?

TARIK

Three wolves. Been there all morning. (She looks. Finds them) How do I know they're still there, with my head in a book? (Sniffs) I smell them. My father your uncle tells me to watch for wolves, he does not tell me how. You think he's so rich he can afford a fool for a son? And don't call me child ...

SURIYA

(Chuckles) All right, I'm sorry, all right? ... (Settles beside him on the ledge, puts an arm round his shoulder, helps herself to cheese) My mother your aunt said they were sending you to the Hakawati School in Ninevah, is that right? (Eats on) I'll call you Hakawati. Hakawati of Ninevah, Teller of the People's History ...

TARIK

I haven't passed my entrance yet...

SURIYA

You will. Everybody knows you were born with an old soul.

TARIK

Maybe. I still have to tell them a story…

SURIYA

The scholars? (He nods) Is that it?

TARIK

(Working on) Ahunh.

SURIYA

Can I read it?

TARIK

It's not for reading. It has to be told…

He flicks back through the revised pages. Closes the book. Stands up on the rock.
Gazes out across the valley, his lips moving in silence as if delivering the tale.

SURIYA

So tell it. (She moves from the rock, sits facing him in the dirt) I'll be the
scholars … (She reworks her scarf into a puffed-up turban; sits formal,
upright; plays with her beard; aged voice) Proceed, Hourani Tarik. It is time
to lay your words upon the air between us. Be sure to speak up. And while
you're at it, remove that silly hat …

TARIK

You're making fun…

SURIYA

(Laughing) No I'm not. Honest. I'm not. (He screws up his nose) I really
want to hear it. (Coaxing) Remember the poems you wrote me, before I
went off to college? I still have them.

TARIK

No you don't. You tore them up in front of me and dropped them on my
shoes…

SURIYA

I was only fifteen, for heaven's sake. I have them in my head.

TARIK

I bet.

SURIYA

Tarik. (He looks at her) Send scorpions to my bed if I tell a lie. I want to hear your story. I love your stories ...

Tarik sniffs, hops down from the rock, restores kuffiah to head, improvises a travel staff, walks around, seeking the zone. She claps her hands, pleased.

TARIK

I haven't started yet ...

He moves out of sight behind the rock, climbs slowly into view, stares around as if at a crowd, bangs the stick ceremonially three times.

TARIK

(Fast, fluent; the standard opening) ... Glory to the One who made the heritage of antiquity a guide for our own time, for it is from this heritage are drawn the tales of the hakawati and all that is in them on fable and adventure ... (Another bang of the stick) One night, in time long gone, while the country languished in the grip of foreign invasion, and plague and famine swept the land like fire on the wind, it came to pass that our ruler Caliph Saddam AlTikriti, beloved Father of the Nation, had a troubling Dream.

He takes out his notebook, checks lines, crosses out. She watches him.

SURIYA

Tarik, you'll change his name, won't you. They'll slaughter you ...

TARIK

(On) ... In the dream his formidable relative Great Aunt Tagrid Hourani, known throughout the North as the Midwife of Tikrit, appeared at the foot of his Bed of State and bade him rise. Take off your shirt, Saddam, she croaked, and stand before the glass, that you may see what you have become. The Caliph meekly did as he was bidden. With her hand the Midwife traced the mounded fat and wasted muscle that hung upon his bones. Where is the bright boy I pulled into this world of joy and pain? How long have you strutted these prideful palace passages, how long have you gorged on rich meats and softened in priceless silks? And now the enemy is at your door, your will and your spirit have crumbled like your flesh, and neither you nor our suffering people will be saved unless you do what I instruct. First, you will leave this place of sin and selfish ease and go back to Tikrit, to the place whence you sprang, to your kin who raised you and to the common folk who taught you all a man needs to know of kindness, of courtesy and of honour. For only thus can you recover your will to do good for the people you rule. As for recovering spirit and body, which lie together like green and blue on a woodpecker's wing, you must then journey alone into the great northern desert, feel the wind on your face, the sun on your back, the sand on your lips, and be as one with yourself and with the nature that gives you life and breath and a pumping heart. And when you have done all this, only then may you return to your palace confident of winning the enduring peace your people ask and your heart will again desire.

He checks the notebook again; makes another edit. Suriya clacks two stones together, unhappy at his drift.

                              TARIK

What? You're bored?

                              SURIYA

Not at all. I'm worried...

                              TARIK

It's too long. I'll cut it...

                              SURIYA

Don't you see...?

                              TARIK

Hear me out. (Bangs the stick. On) The next morning, while his counsellors waited for their usual meeting, the Caliph wrote a short note of instruction to his Vizier, slipped from the Palace, saddled a horse and set out for the north. Of the days and nights he spent there in Tikrit, of hard work and simple pleasure, of the truths he learned again from the common folk, of the goodness and courtesy of villagers at one with their lives, the scribes of all ages have had abundant say and need not detain us. Enough to say, when he came to the end of his stay there, his will once again strong and clear, he knew absolutely the dream was real and must be followed to its end.

With a camel bought from a travelling Sudani, a tent and provisions from the tiny suk, maps of the waterholes and the night skies, he set out alone, lit only by the moon, on the journey that would make him a man again at one with his life and with the world of nature he had all but forgotten. But if the dream was real, so was the camel. On the second night it took him an hour to haul it to its feet and get it moving. On the third, he had to walk ahead and drag it. On the fourth it collapsed in an untidy heap in the sand as if dead. The sun rose and still it did not move, beat it all he may. And fear trickled into his heart like boiling fat. And questions flicked at his brain like the tongues of lizards. What am I doing here? How can the dream be real if I am to die alone in the wilderness? How could I buy a camel from a bloody travelling Sudani ...? (Suriya yelps. He grins at her) The Man from Tikrit scans the empty horizon, left, right, before, behind. Nothing. And yet not quite nothing. On top of a large dune some way off something green, something flapping in the breeze, something flapping greenly up ahead. He grabs his water bottle and scrambles up the slope. And slowly as he climbs, it comes into view, a large green tent, a small green flag flapping from its roof, and on the tent a sign which reads alHourani – Camel Station. Is it a mirage, the tricks of the desert, he asked himself? How can this be real? As if in answer, a man dressed in faded boiler suit and wiping his hands on an oily rag appears in the doorway. Welcome, brother, he calls. Come inside, I'll make some tea, you look like a man with a problem.

TARIK (cont)

Are you ... the owner? asks the Man from Tikrit. Abdel Hourani, at your service. How can I help? We do full service, top-up, repairs and parts. You do have a camel, do you? Broke down, bottom of the hill, says the Caliph. Right, you'll need recovery, then. He whistles up his two boys and off they go to bring in the camel. Inside the tent, while Hourani mashes sweet green tea from Jericho, the Caliph finds his eyes drawn upwards to the roof of the tent, where a maze of sacred and profane texts have been painted in gold leaf on the green canvas. And at the very heart of the maze, six lines from the great epic of Gilgamesh, first of earthly kings, builder of the first city, which he had learned from his mother and long since forgotten. *Be what you are. Seek not what you may not find. Let your every day be full of joy. Love the child that holds your hand. Let your wife delight in your embrace. For these alone are the concerns of humanity.* How can this be real? he asks aloud. How can it not? replies Hourani, handing him the tea. Your camel's on its way, drink up, there's work to do. At length the boys return, dragging the beast behind them, and Hourani takes it into the workshop to look it over. Ahunh, he says, I can fix this, no problem. Place him over the inspection pit. When the camel's in position he climbs down into the pit to take a closer look. The Man from Tikrit looks on, amazed. Do you know whose life it is you're saving, he whispers. Uhunh, answers Hourani, studying the job. Your Caliph's, Saddam alTikriti's, that's whose life you're saving. Is that right, says the man. Well well well. Hand me those two stones, will you. Saddam hands him the stones, Hourani takes one in each palm and lines up the camel's testicles between them ...

SURIYA

(Shrieking) Tarik! You can't ..!!

TARIK

... and Bang!!! The camel leaps two feet into the air with a mighty bellow and shoots off to the horizon like a Saudi racehorse ...

Suriya shrieks again, her frame wracked with laughter. Tarik sniffs, turns to look across at the wolf ledge up the hill.

TARIK

They've gone ... (Sudden, loud) DOWN!

He leaps to shield her, seconds before an F15 screams past, two hundred feet above their heads. Displaced air pounds around the space, the noise slowly drains to nothing. Tarik helps her to her feet. Disturbed shouts, bleats, from down the hill.

TARIK

You all right?

SURIYA

God save us.

TARIK

They do worse than that sometimes. Maybe he did.

He brushes hair and dust from her face with a finger. A man's call from below: Suriya! Are you all right? Get down here now. Get down here, girl. She smiles at Tarik.

SURIYA

(Calling) Coming, poppa ... (Tarik returns to sit on rock ledge) I have to go ... (He nods) Is there much more? (He shakes his head) Go on then...

Another huge shout from below.

SURIYA

(Loud) I'm coming, poppa. On my way.

She shrugs her shoulders, makes a rueful face, begins to thread her way down the slope. He follows to watch her go.

> TARIK
>
> (After her) … There you are, Caliph, says Hourani, all fixed and up and running. What do you mean, screams alTikriti, how in God's name am I going to catch him? Not a problem, says Hourani. Get over the pit …

He listens to her laughter trailing back up the hill. Smiles. Frowns, hearing something.

> TARIK
>
> (Loud) Coming BACK!!!

The plane screams back, a hundred feet further down the hill. Rafts of bullets smash into the hillside. Gone. Smoke, dust, groans, men, sheep. Tarik gets to his feet, rage and fear at war in his slender frame.

> TARIK
>
> (Calling) Poppa. Suriya. Are you there? I'm all right. (He looks down. The groans fade. He shakes his head, wipes his face with his hand. Stares up at the sky. Takes out his Yankees cap, throws it with venom, up and out) No more Yankees, Yankee. (Scrabbles his book from a pocket. Does the same) No more stories.

He picks up his rifle, holds it above his head. Lights fade.

Thoughts about America and the Future

Edward Said

Professor Said teaches at Columbia University in the United States. His recent books, The Edward Said Reader and Reflections on Exile and other Literary and Cultural Essays, are published in Britain by Granta.

I

I don't know a single Arab or Muslim American who does not now feel that he or she belongs to the enemy camp, and that being in the United States at this moment provides us with an especially unpleasant experience of alienation and widespread, quite specifically targeted hostility. For despite the occasional official statements saying that Islam and Muslims and Arabs are not enemies of the United States, everything else about the current situation argues the exact opposite.

Hundreds of young Arab and Muslim men have been picked up for questioning and, in far too many cases, detained by the police or the Federal Bureau of Investigation. Anyone with an Arab or Muslim name is usually made to stand aside for special attention during airport security checks. There have been many reported instances of discriminatory behaviour against Arabs, so that speaking Arabic or even reading an Arabic document in public is likely to draw unwelcome attention. And of course, the media have run far too many 'experts' and 'commentators' on terrorism, Islam, and the Arabs whose endlessly repetitious and reductive line is so hostile and so misrepresents our history, society and culture that the media itself has become little more than an arm of the war on terrorism in Afghanistan and elsewhere, as now seems to be the case with the projected attack to 'end' Iraq. There are US forces already in several countries with important Muslim populations like the Philippines and Somalia, the build-up against Iraq continues, and Israel prolongs its sadistic collective punishment of the Palestinian people, all with what seems like great public approval in the United States.

While true in some respects, this is quite misleading. America is more than what Bush and Rumsfeld and the others say it is. I have come to deeply resent the notion that I must accept the picture of America as being involved in a 'just war' against something unilaterally labelled as terrorism by Bush and his advisers, a war that has assigned us the role of either silent witnesses or defensive immigrants who should be grateful to be allowed residence in the United States. The historical realities are different: America is an immigrant republic and has always been one. It is a nation of laws passed not by God but by its citizens. Except for the mostly exterminated native Americans, the original Indians, everyone who now lives here as an American citizen originally came to these shores as an immigrant from somewhere else, even Bush and Rumsfeld. The Constitution does not provide for different levels of Americanness, nor for approved or disapproved forms of 'American behaviour,' including things that have come to be called 'un-' or 'anti- American' statements or attitudes. That is the invention of American Taliban who want to regulate speech and behaviour in ways that remind one eerily of the un-regretted former rulers of Afghanistan. And even if Mr Bush insists on the importance of religion in America, he is not authorised to enforce such views on the citizenry or to speak for everyone when he makes proclamations in China and elsewhere about God and America and himself. The Constitution expressly separates church and state.

There is worse. By passing the Patriot Act last November, Bush and his compliant Congress have suppressed or abrogated or abridged whole sections of the First, Fourth, Fifth and Eighth Amendments, instituted legal procedures that give individuals no recourse either to a proper defence or a fair trial, that allow secret searches, eavesdropping, detention without limit, and, given the treatment of the prisoners at Guantanamo Bay, that allow the United States executive branch to abduct prisoners, detain them indefinitely, decide unilaterally whether or not they are prisoners of war and whether or not the Geneva Conventions apply to them – which is not a decision to be taken by individual countries. Moreover, as Congressman Dennis Kucinich (Democrat, Ohio) said in a magnificent speech given on 17 February, the president and his men were not authorised to declare war (Operation Enduring Freedom) against the world without limit or reason, were not authorised to increase military spending to over $400 billion per year, were not authorised to repeal the Bill of Rights. Furthermore, he added – the first such statement by a prominent, publicly elected official – 'we did not ask that the blood of innocent people, who perished on September 11, be avenged with the blood of innocent villagers in Afghanistan.' I strongly recommend that Rep. Kucinich's speech, which was made with the best of American principles and values in mind, be published in full in Arabic so that people in our part of the world can understand that America is not a monolith for the use of George Bush and Dick Cheney, but in fact contains many voices and currents of opinion which this government is trying to silence or make irrelevant.

The problem for the world today is how to deal with the unparalleled and unprecedented power of the United States, which in effect has made no secret of the fact that it does not need co-ordination with or approval of others in the pursuit of what a small circle of men and women around Bush believe are its interests. So far as the Middle East is concerned, it does seem that since 11 September there has been almost an Israelisation of United States policy: and in effect Ariel Sharon and his associates have cynically exploited the single-minded attention to 'terrorism' by George Bush and have used that as a cover for their continued failed policy against the Palestinians. The point here is that Israel is not the United States and, mercifully, the US is not Israel: thus, even though Israel commands Bush's support for the moment, Israel is a small country whose continued survival as an ethnocentric state in the midst of an Arab-Islamic sea depends not just on an expedient if not infinite dependence on the United States, but rather on accommodation with its environment, not the other way round. That is why I think Sharon's policy has finally been revealed to a significant number of Israelis as suicidal, and why more and more Israelis are taking the reserve officers' position against serving the military occupation as a model for their approach and resistance. This is the best thing to have emerged from the *Intifada*. It proves that Palestinian courage and defiance in resisting occupation have finally brought fruit.

What has not changed, however, is the United States position, which has been escalating towards a more and more metaphysical sphere, in which Bush and his people identify themselves (as in the very name of the military campaign, Operation Enduring Freedom) with righteousness, purity, the good, and manifest destiny, its external enemies with an equally absolute evil. Anyone reading the world press in the past few weeks can ascertain that people outside the United States are both mystified by and aghast at the vagueness of US policy, which claims for itself the right to imagine and create enemies on a world scale, then prosecute wars on them without much regard for accuracy of definition, specificity of aim, concreteness of goal, or, worst of all, the legality of such actions. What does it mean to defeat 'evil terrorism' in a world like ours? It cannot mean eradicating everyone who opposes the United States, an infinite and strangely pointless task; nor can it mean changing the world map to suit the United States, substituting people we think are 'good guys' for evil creatures like Saddam Hussein. The radical simplicity of all this is attractive to Washington bureaucrats whose domain is either purely theoretical or who, because they sit behind desks in the Pentagon, tend to see the world as a distant target for the United State's very real and virtually unopposed power. For if you live 10,000 miles away from any known evil state and you have at your disposal acres of warplanes, 19 aircraft carriers, and dozens of submarines, plus a million and a half people under arms, all of them willing to serve their country idealistically in the pursuit of what Bush and Condoleezza Rice keep referring to as evil, the chances are that you will be willing to use all that power sometime, somewhere, especially if the administration keeps asking for (and getting) billions of dollars to be added to the already swollen defence budget.

From my point of view, the most shocking thing of all is that with few exceptions most prominent intellectuals and commentators in this country have tolerated the Bush programme, tolerated and in some flagrant cases, tried to go beyond it, toward more self- righteous sophistry, more uncritical self-flattery, more specious argument. What they will not accept is that the world we live in, the historical world of nations and peoples, is moved and can be understood by politics, not by huge general absolutes like good and evil, with America always on the side of good, its enemies on the side of evil. When Thomas Friedman tiresomely sermonises to Arabs that they have to be more self-critical, missing in anything he says is the slightest tone of self- criticism. Somehow, he thinks, the atrocities of 11 September entitle him to preach at others, as if only the United States had suffered such terrible losses, and as if lives lost elsewhere in the world were not worth lamenting quite as much or drawing as large moral conclusions from.

One notices the same discrepancies and blindness when Israeli intellectuals concentrate on their own tragedies and leave out of the equation the much greater suffering of a dispossessed people without a state, or an army, or an air force, or a proper leadership, that is, Palestinians whose suffering at the hands of Israel continues minute by minute, hour by hour. This sort of moral blindness, this inability to evaluate and weigh the comparative evidence of sinner and sinned against (to use a moralistic language that I normally avoid and detest) is very much the order of the day, and it must be the critical intellectual's job not to fall into – indeed, actively to campaign against falling into – the trap. It is not enough to say blandly that all human suffering is equal, then to go on basically bewailing one's own miseries: it is far more important to see what the strongest party does, and to question rather than justify that. The intellectual's is a voice in opposition to and critical of great power, which is consistently in need of a restraining and clarifying conscience and a comparative perspective, so that the victim will not, as is often the case, be blamed and real power encouraged to do its will.

A week ago I was stunned when a European friend asked me what I thought of a declaration by 60 American intellectuals that was published in all the major French, German, Italian and other continental papers but which did not appear in the United States at all, except on the Internet where few people took notice of it. This declaration took the form of a pompous sermon about the American war against evil and terrorism being 'just' and in keeping with American values, as defined by these self-appointed interpreters of our country. Paid for and sponsored by something called the Institute for American Values, whose main (and financially well-endowed) aim is to propagate ideas in favour of families, 'fathering' and 'mothering,' and God, the declaration was signed by Samuel Huntington, Francis Fukuyama, Daniel Patrick Moynihan among many others, but basically written by a conservative feminist academic, Jean Bethke Elshtain. Its main arguments about a 'just' war were inspired by Professor Michael Walzer, a supposed socialist who is allied with the pro-Israel lobby in this country, and whose role is to justify everything Israel does by recourse to vaguely leftist principles. In signing this declaration, Walzer has given up all pretension to leftism and, like Sharon, allies himself with an interpretation (and a questionable one at that) of America as a righteous warrior against terror and evil, the more to make it appear that Israel and the US are similar countries with similar aims.

Nothing could be further from the truth, since Israel is not the state of its citizens but of all the Jewish people, while the United States is most assuredly only the state of its citizens. Moreover, Walzer never has the courage to state boldly that in supporting Israel he is supporting a state structured by ethno-religious principles, which (with typical hypocrisy) he would oppose in the United States if this country were declared to be white and Christian.

Walzer's inconsistencies and hypocrisies aside, the document is really addressed to 'our Muslim brethren' who are supposed to understand that America's war is not against Islam but against those who oppose all sorts of principles, which it would be hard to disagree with. Who could oppose the principle that all human beings are equal, that killing in the name of God is a bad thing, that freedom of conscience is excellent, and that 'the basic subject of society is the human person, and the legitimate role of government is to protect and help to foster the conditions for human flourishing'? In what follows, however, America turns out to be the aggrieved party and, even though some of its mistakes in policy are acknowledged very briefly (and without mentioning anything specific in detail), it is depicted as hewing to principles unique to the United States, such as that all people possess inherent moral dignity and status, that universal moral truths exist and are available to everyone, or that civility is important where there is disagreement, and that freedom of conscience and religion are a reflection of basic human dignity and are universally recognised. Fine. For although the authors of this sermon say it is often the case that such great principles are contravened, no sustained attempt is made to say where and when those contraventions actually occur (as they do all the time), or whether they have been more contravened than followed, or anything as concrete as that. Yet in a long footnote, Walzer and his colleagues set forth a list of how many American 'murders' have occurred at Muslim and Arab hands, including those of the Marines in Beirut in 1983, as well as other military combatants.

Somehow making a list of that kind is worth making for these militant defenders of America, whereas the murder of Arabs and Muslims – including the hundreds of thousands killed with American weapons by Israel with United States support, or the hundreds of thousands killed by US-maintained sanctions against the innocent civilian population of Iraq – need be neither mentioned nor tabulated. What sort of dignity is there in humiliating Palestinians by Israel, with American complicity and even co-operation, and where is the nobility and moral conscience of saying nothing as Palestinian children are killed, millions besieged, and millions more kept as stateless refugees? Or for that matter, the millions killed in Vietnam, Columbia, Turkey, and Indonesia with American support and acquiescence?

All in all, this declaration of principles and complaint addressed by American intellectuals to their Muslim brethren seems like neither a statement of real conscience nor of true intellectual criticism against the arrogant use of power, but rather is the opening salvo in a new cold war declared by the United States in full ironic co-operation, it would seem, with those Islamists who have argued that 'our' war is with the West and with America. Speaking as someone with a claim on America and the Arabs, I find this sort of hijacking rhetoric profoundly objectionable. While it pretends to the elucidation of principles and the declaration of values, it is in fact exactly the opposite, an exercise in not knowing, in blinding readers with a patriotic rhetoric that encourages ignorance as it overrides real politics, real history, and real moral issues. Despite its vulgar trafficking in great 'principles and values,' it does none of that, except to wave them around in a bullying way designed to cow foreign readers into submission. I have a feeling that this document wasn't published here for two reasons: one is that it would be so severely criticised by American readers that it would be laughed out of court and two, that it was designed as part of a recently announced, extremely well-funded Pentagon scheme to put out propaganda as part of the war effort, and therefore intended for foreign consumption.

Whatever the case, the publication of 'What are American Values?' augurs a new and degraded era in the production of intellectual discourse. For when the intellectuals of the most powerful country in the history of the world align themselves so flagrantly with that power, pressing that power's case instead of urging restraint, reflection, genuine communication and understanding, we are back to the bad old days of the intellectual war against communism, which we now know brought far too many compromises, collaborations and fabrications on the part of intellectuals and artists who should have played an altogether different role. Subsidised and underwritten by the government (the Central Intelligence Agency especially, which went as far as providing for the subvention of magazines like *Encounter*, underwrote scholarly research, travel and concerts as well as artistic exhibitions), those militantly unreflective and uncritical intellectuals and artists in the 1950s and 1960s brought to the whole notion of intellectual honesty and complicity a new and disastrous dimension. For along with that effort went also the domestic campaign to stifle debate, intimidate critics, and restrict thought. For many Americans, like myself, this is a shameful episode in our history, and we must be on our guard against and resist its return.

II
Thinking ahead: after survival, what happens?

Anyone with any connection at all to Palestine is today (7 April 2002) in a state of stunned outrage and shock. While almost a repeat of what happened in 1982, Israel's current all-out colonial assault on the Palestinian people (with George Bush's astoundingly ignorant and grotesque support) is indeed worse than Sharon's two previous mass forays in 1971 and 1982 against the Palestinian people. The political and moral climate today is a good deal cruder and reductive, the media's destructive role (which has played the part almost entirely of singling out Palestinian suicide attacks and isolating them from their context in Israel's 35-year illegal occupation of the Palestinian territories) greater in favouring the Israeli view of things, the United States' power more unchallenged, the war against terrorism has more completely taken over the global agenda and, so far as the Arab environment is concerned, there is greater incoherence and fragmentation than ever before.

Sharon's homicidal instincts have been enhanced (if that's the right word) by all of the above, and magnified to boot. This in effect means that he can do more damage with more impunity than before, although he is also more deeply undermined than before in all his efforts as well as in his entire career by the failure that comes with single-minded negation and hate, which in the end nourish neither political nor even military success. Conflicts between peoples such as this contain more elements than can be eliminated by tanks and air power, and a war against unarmed civilians – no matter how many times Sharon lumberingly and mindlessly trumpets his stupid mantras about terror – can never bring a really lasting political result of the sort his dreams tells him he can have. Palestinians will not go away. Besides, Sharon will almost certainly end up disgraced and rejected by his people. He has no plan, except to destroy everything about Palestine and the Palestinians. Even in his enraged fixation on Arafat and terror, he is failing to do much more than raise the man's prestige while essentially drawing attention to the blind monomania of his own position.

In the end he is Israel's problem to deal with. For us, our main consideration now is morally to do everything in our power to make certain that despite the enormous suffering and destruction imposed on us by a criminal war, we must go on. When a renowned and respected retired politician like Zbigniew Brzezinski says explicitly on national television that Israel has been behaving like the white supremacist regime of apartheid South Africa, one can be certain that he is not alone in this view, and that an increasing number of Americans and others are slowly growing not only disenchanted but also disgusted with Israel as a hugely expensive and draining ward of the United States, costing far too much, increasing American isolation, and seriously damaging the country's reputation with its allies and its citizens. The question is what, in this most difficult of moments, can we rationally learn about the present crisis that we need to include in our plans for the future?

What I have to say now is highly selective, but it is the modest fruit of many years working on behalf of the Palestinian cause as someone who is from both Arab and Western worlds. I neither know nor can say everything, but here are some of the handful of thoughts I can contribute at this very difficult hour. Each of the four points that follow here is related to the other.

First, for better or for worse, Palestine is not just an Arab and Islamic cause, it is important to many different, contradictory and yet intersecting worlds. To work for Palestine is necessarily to be aware of these many dimensions and constantly to educate oneself in them. For that we need a highly educated, vigilant and sophisticated leadership and democratic support for it. Above all we must, as Mandela never tired of saying about his struggle, be aware that Palestine is one of the great moral causes of our time. Therefore, we need to treat it as such. It's not a matter of trade, or bartering negotiations, or making a career. It is a just cause which should allow Palestinians to capture the high moral ground and keep it.

Second, there are different kinds of power, military of course being the most obvious. What has enabled Israel to do what it has been doing to the Palestinians for the past 54 years is the result of a carefully and scientifically planned campaign to validate Israeli actions and, simultaneously, devalue and efface Palestinian actions. This is not just a matter of maintaining a powerful military but of organising opinion, especially in the United States and Western Europe, and is a power derived from slow, methodical work where Israel's position is seen as one to be easily identified with, whereas the Palestinians are thought of as Israel's enemies, hence repugnant, dangerous, against 'us.' Since the end of the Cold War, Europe has faded into near-insignificance so far as the organisation of opinion, images, and thought are concerned. America (outside of Palestine itself) is the main arena of battle. We have simply never learned the importance of systematically organising our political work in this country on a mass level, so that for instance the average American will not immediately think of 'terrorism' when the word 'Palestinian' is pronounced. That kind of work quite literally protects whatever gains we might have made through on-the-ground resistance to Israel's occupation. What has enabled Israel to deal with us with impunity, therefore, has been that we are unprotected by any body of opinion that would deter Sharon from practising his war crimes and saying that what he has done is to fight terrorism. Given the immense diffusive, insistent, and repetitive power of the images broadcast by CNN, for example, in which the phrase 'suicide bomb' is numbingly repeated a hundred times an hour for the American consumer and tax-payer, it is the grossest negligence not to have had a team of people like Hanan Ashrawi, Leila Shahid, Ghassan Khatib, Afif Safie – to mention just a few – sitting in Washington ready to go on CNN or any of the other channels just to tell the Palestinian story, provide context and understanding, give us a moral and narrative presence with positive, rather than merely negative, value. We need a future leadership that understands this as one of the basic lessons of modern politics in an age of electronic communication. Not to have understood this is part of the tragedy of today.

Third, there is simply no use operating politically and responsibly in a world dominated by one superpower without a profound familiarity and knowledge of that superpower – America, its history, its institutions, its currents and counter-currents, its politics and culture; and, above all, a perfect working knowledge of its language. To hear our spokesmen, as well as the other Arabs, saying the most ridiculous things about America, throwing themselves on its mercy, cursing it in one breath, asking for its help in another, all in miserably inadequate fractured English, shows a state of such primitive incompetence as to make one cry. America is not monolithic. We have friends and we have possible friends. We can cultivate, mobilise, and use our communities and their affiliated communities here as an integral part of our politics of liberation, just as the South Africans did, or as the Algerians did in France during their struggle for liberation. Planning, discipline, co-ordination. We have not at all understood the politics of non-violence. Moreover, neither have we understood the power of trying to address Israelis directly, the way the African National Congress addressed the white South Africans, as part of a politics of inclusion and mutual respect. Coexistence is our answer to Israeli exclusivism and belligerence. This is not conceding: it is creating solidarity, and therefore isolating the exclusivists, the racists, the fundamentalists.

Fourth, the most important lesson of all for us to understand about ourselves is manifest in the terrible tragedies of what Israel is now doing in the occupied territories. The fact is that we are a people and a society, and despite Israel's ferocious attack against the Palestinian Authority, our society still functions. We are a people because we have a functioning society which goes on – and has gone on for the past 54 years – despite every sort of abuse, every cruel turn of history, every misfortune we have suffered, every tragedy we have gone through as a people. Our greatest victory over Israel is that people like Sharon and his kind do not have the capacity to see that, and this is why they are doomed despite their great power and their awful, inhuman cruelty. We have surmounted the tragedies and memories of our past, whereas such Israelis as Sharon have not. He will go to his grave only as an Arab-killer, and a failed politician who brought more unrest and insecurity to his people. It must surely be the legacy of a leader that he should leave something behind upon which future generations will build. Sharon, Mofaz, and all the others associated with them in this bullying, sadistic campaign of death and carnage will have left nothing except gravestones. Negation breeds negation.

As Palestinians, I think we can say that we left a vision and a society that has survived every attempt to kill it. And that is something. It is for the generation of my children and yours, to go on from there, critically, rationally, with hope and forbearance.

Not in
Our Name

John Pilger

*John Pilger's investigative
journalism and
documentary films are
widely acclaimed. His latest
book, The New Rulers of
the World, is published by
Verso.*

How dare George Bush preach peace to Israel when he met Blair to plan war on Iraq and the deaths of thousands more innocent people?

President Bush called on Israel to withdraw from the Palestinian cities occupied by its forces. He excused Israel's violence, but lectured the Palestinians and the rest of the Middle East on the need for restraint and a lasting peace. 'The storms of violence cannot go on,' said Bush. 'Enough is enough.'

What he neglected to say was that he needs a lull in the present crisis to lay his own war plans; that while he talks of peace in the Middle East, he is secretly planning a massive attack on Iraq. This historic display of hypocrisy by Bush was on show at his ranch in Texas, with Tony Blair, his collaborator, in admiring attendance. Yes, enough is enough. It is time Tony Blair came clean with the British people on his part in the coming violence against a nation of innocent people.

As the crisis in Israeli-occupied Palestine deepened, Tony Blair met George W Bush to plan an attack on Iraq. Their decision may condemn to death more than 10,000 civilians. That is the 'medium case scenario' drawn up by the Pentagon. If the Americans implement their current strategy of 'total war' and target Iraq's electricity and water, the consequences will be even more horrific. There is no mandate in any United Nations resolution for this invasion. It will be as lawless as Nazi Germany's invasion of Poland, which triggered the Second World War. Indeed, it may well trigger a Third World War, drawing in nations of the region and beyond.

As Blair arrived at Bush's Texas ranch the question begged: Why did he condemn Iraq, but remain silent on Israel's current bloody and illegal rampage through Palestine? Why has he not demanded that the Israeli Prime Minister Ariel Sharon comply with United Nations Security Council resolutions, to which Britain is a signatory, and withdraw from the Occupied

Territories? Why has Blair said nothing as Sharon has sent tanks and gunships and snipers against civilians — a government targeting innocent people, like the deaf old lady shot by an Israeli sniper as she tried to get to hospital? Why has Blair not called at least for military sanctions against Israel, which has 200 nuclear weapons targeted at Arab capitals?

Blair's culpable silence is imposed by the most dangerous American administration for a generation. The Bush administration is determined to attack Iraq and take over a country that is the world's second largest source of oil. The aim is to get rid of America's and Britain's old friend, Saddam Hussein, whom they no longer control, and to install another compliant thug in Baghdad. *That* is why Bush now tells Israel to withdraw from the Palestinian cities it recently occupied while continuing to replenish the Israeli war machine. The Americans want a rampant Israel guarding their flank as they attack Iraq and expand their control across the Middle East, whose oil is now more critical than ever to United States military and economic dominance.

For almost two months, Downing Street, through the discredited system of unattributable briefings that are secret to the public, have spun two deceptions. The first is that the Prime Minister was to play a vital role at the meeting with Bush on his Texas ranch in 'counselling caution.' The second is that Blair has a 'dossier of detailed evidence' that 'proves' that Saddam Hussein has 'a nuclear capability' and is 'investigating a way to launch unsophisticated nuclear bombs' and is also building chemical and biological weapons. The fiction of Blair as a steadying hand on his Texas buddy is to be read in Blair's unrelenting bellicose statements, and his attempts, against the wishes of his senior military advisers, to send thousands of British troops into the quagmire of Afghanistan, where his 'cautionary influence' on Bush saw as many as 5,000 civilians bombed to death while the Taliban and al-Qaeda leaders got away.

While remaining silent on Israel, Blair is alone in Europe in his promotion of an attack on Iraq, a nation of 22 million people with whom the British have no quarrel. Mysteriously, the 'dossier of proof' of the dangers posed by the Iraqi regime has now been 'shelved.' This is because no such proof exists and because, suddenly, more than 130 Labour Members of Parliament are in revolt, including Cabinet and former Cabinet members. It must be dawning on many of them that so much of this government's 'spin' during the 'war on terrorism' has been a farrago of lies and half-truths provided by an American intelligence apparatus seeking to cover its failure to provide warning of the attacks of September 11.

Lie Number One is the justification for an attack on Iraq — the threat of its 'weapons of mass destruction.' Few countries have had 93 per cent of their major weapons capability destroyed. This was reported by Rolf Ekeus, the chairman of the United Nations body authorised to inspect and destroy Iraq's arsenal following the Gulf War in 1991. United Nations inspectors certified that 817 out of the 819 Iraqi long-range missiles were destroyed. In 1999, a special panel of the Security Council recorded that Iraq's main biological weapons facilities (supplied originally by the United States and Britain) 'have been destroyed and rendered harmless.'

As for Saddam Hussein's 'nuclear threat,' the International Atomic Energy Agency reported that Iraq's nuclear weapons programme had been eliminated 'efficiently and effectively'. The Agency's inspectors still travel to Iraq and in January reported full Iraqi compliance. Blair and Bush never mention this when they demand that 'the weapons inspectors are allowed back'. Nor do they remind us that the United Nations inspectors were never expelled by the Iraqis, but withdrawn only after it was revealed they had been infiltrated by United States intelligence.

Lie Number Two is the connection between Iraq and the perpetrators of September 11. There was the rumour that Mohammed Atta, one of the September 11 hijackers, had met an Iraqi intelligence official in the Czech Republic last year. The Czech police say he was not even in the country last year. On February 5, a *New York Times* investigation concluded: 'The Central Intelligence Agency has no evidence that Iraq has engaged in terrorist operations against the United States in nearly a decade, and the Agency is convinced that Saddam Hussein has not provided chemical or biological weapons to al-Qaeda or related terrorist groups.'

Lie Number Three is that Saddam Hussein, not the United States and Britain, 'is blocking humanitarian supplies from reaching the people of Iraq.' (Foreign Office minister Peter Hain). The opposite is true. The United States, with British compliance, is currently blocking a record $5billion worth of humanitarian supplies from the people of Iraq. These are shipments already approved by the United Nations Office of Iraq, which is authorised by the Security Council. They include life-saving drugs, painkillers, vaccines, and cancer diagnostic equipment.

This wanton denial is rarely reported in Britain. Hundreds of thousands of Iraqis, mostly children, have died as a consequence of an American and British driven embargo on Iraq that resembles a medieval siege. The embargo allows Iraq less than £100 with which to feed and care for one person for a whole year. This a major factor, says the United Nations' Children's Fund, in the deaths of more than 600,000 infants.

I have seen the appalling state of the children of Iraq. I have sat next to an Iraqi doctor in a modern hospital while she has turned away parents with children suffering from cancers that are part of what they call a 'Hiroshima epidemic' — caused, according to several studies, by the depleted uranium that was used by the United States and Britain in the Gulf War and is now carried in the dust of the desert. Not only is Iraq denied equipment to clean up its contaminated battlefields, but also cancer drugs and hospital equipment.

I showed a list of barred drugs given to me by Iraqi doctors to Professor Karol Sikora who, as chief of the cancer programme of the World Health Organisation, wrote in the *British Medical Journal*: 'Requested radiotherapy equipment, chemotherapy drugs and analgesics are consistently blocked by United States and British advisers (to the United Nations Sanctions Committee). There seems to be a rather ludicrous notion that such agents could be converted into chemical and other weapons.' He told me: 'Nearly all these drugs are available in every British hospital. It seems crazy they couldn't have morphine. When I was in Iraq, in one hospital they had a little bottle of aspirin pills to go around 200 patients in pain.' No one doubts that if the murderous Saddam Hussein saw advantage in deliberately denying his people humanitarian supplies, he would do so; but the United Nations, from the Secretary General himself, has said that, while the regime could do more, it has not withheld supplies.

Denis Halliday, the assistant Secretary General of the United Nations, resigned in protest at the embargo which he described as 'genocidal'. Halliday was responsible for the United Nation's humanitarian programme in Iraq. His successor, Hans Von Sponeck, also resigned in disgust. Last November, they wrote: 'The death of 5-6,000 children a month is mostly due to contaminated water, lack of medicines and malnutrition. The United States and United Kingdom governments' delayed clearance of equipment and materials is responsible for this tragedy, not Baghdad.'

Those who speak these facts are abused by Blair's ministers as apologists for Saddam Hussein — so embroiled is the government with the Bush administration's exploitation of America's own tragedy on September 11. This has prevented public discussion of the crime of an embargo that has hurt only the most vulnerable Iraqis and which is to be compounded by the crime of attacking the stricken nation. Unknown to most of the British public, RAF and American aircraft have been bombing Iraq, week after week, for more than two years. The cost to the British taxpayer is £800million a year. The *Wall Street Journal* reported that the United States and Britain faced a 'dilemma' because 'few targets remain'. 'We're down to the last outhouse,' said a Pentagon official.

In any attack on Iraq, Saddam Hussein's escape route is virtually assured — just as Osama bin Laden's was. The United States and Britain have no wish to free the Iraqi people from a tyranny the Central Intelligence Agency once described as its 'greatest triumph'. The last thing they want is a separate Kurdish state and another allied to the Shi'ite majority in neighbouring Iran. They want another Saddam Hussein: one who will do as he is told. On March 13, the Foreign Office entertained Brigadier-General Najib Salihi, a former commander of Saddam Hussein's Republican Guard and chief of the dreaded military intelligence who took part in the invasion of Kuwait in 1990. Now funded by the Central Intelligence Agency, the general 'denies any war crimes'. Not that he would ever face arrest in the West. At the Foreign Office, he is known as a 'rapidly rising star'. He is their man, and Washington's man.

The British soldiers who take part in an invasion have every right to know the dirty secrets that will underpin their action, and extend the suffering of a people held hostage to a dictatorship and to international power games over which they have no control. The Americans have made clear they are prepared to use 'low yield' nuclear weapons, a threat echoed here by Defence Secretary Geoffrey Hoon.

When will Europe stand up? If the leaders of the European Union fall silent, too, in the face of such danger, what is Europe for? In this country, there is an honourable rallying cry: Not In Our Name. Bush and Blair must be restrained from killing large numbers of innocents in our name — a view, according to the polls, shared by a majority of the British people. An arms and military equipment embargo must be enforced throughout the region, from Saddam Hussein's Iraq to Ariel Sharon's Israel. Above all, the siege of both the Iraqi and Palestinian peoples must end now.

ASLEF sends Mayday greetings to all members of the trade union and Labour movement

Say yes to an immediate withdrawal of Israeli troops from the occupied territories

Support Palestine by demanding the implementation of UN resolutions 242 and 338

Say no to any attempts to invade Iraq

Post-Labour's New Imperialism

Ken Coates

Reordering the World, The Long-term Implications of 11 September, edited by Mark Leonard with a foreword by Tony Blair, is published by the Foreign Policy Centre. It features thirteen other papers besides that of Robert Cooper, considered here.

Ken Coates was a member of the European Parliament from 1989 to 1999. He is the editor of The Spokesman and chairman of the Bertrand Russell Peace Foundation.

Robert Cooper, who is said to be not without influence in Downing Street, is the author of what has been proposed as a keynote text for British foreign policy, published under the general title *Reordering the World*. This is presented with a foreword by Tony Blair, who thinks that it, and the essays which accompany it, add up to a blueprint 'for a more secure, prosperous and just world'. The bizarrely miscalled 'war on terror' will, while such blueprints multiply, cause disorder, civilian deaths, and general mayhem to multiply with them; but whether they will conduce to security or prosperity among the warriors remains to be seen. Justice will be nowhere in evidence. That is why this paper provokes sour responses. It has already moved Tam Dalyell to give his judgement: 'The Tsarina of Russia was better advised by Rasputin than the Prime Minister is by this maniac'. However, Mr. Cooper surely knows his Tsarina, and has had more sense than counsel her against her own ample prejudices.

Cooper identifies 1989 as the end not only of the Cold War, but also of a European state system which had endured from the time of the Thirty Years War onwards. Conveniently, he achieves topicality for this thought by claiming that 'September 11th (2001) showed us one of the implications' of this agenda.

Cooper's assumption is that international order has heretofore been based on either hegemony or balance. The two concepts have not been mutually exclusive: empires may have been 'generally static', but the more that they have established security zones within themselves, the greater has been their need to maintain balance all around them. It is not necessary to follow this argument through the detail of recent history. But most of us will recognise a degree of truth in it.

Cooper's world contains a 'pre-modern' zone of semi-anarchic states, many of them former colonies, in which the rule of law scarcely exists. He cites countries such as

Somalia and 'until recently' Afghanistan. Probably this caveat about Afghanistan will prove to be unjustified, since, in spite of noisy boasts to the contrary, there is no sign whatever of the establishment of a stable state in that unfortunate country.

The second zone identified by Cooper is that of 'post-imperial, post-modern states who no longer think of security primarily in terms of conquest'. This zone includes the European Union, Canada and probably Japan. It does not include the United States, which slips off the map altogether. This is the central flaw in Cooper's argument. Hamlet, indeed, without the Prince.

We are left with the third zone of 'traditional "modern" states'. These behave as states always have, following Machiavellian principles of *raison d'état*. Cooper thinks of India, Pakistan and China in this category, but it is difficult to see why. The Pakistan Government tumbles in and out of military dictatorship, and is now under the direct suzerainty of the United States. India is more and more openly a client of the United States. And China has the honour of being the major league enemy of the United States, insofar as the advance of trade and business permit.

The taxonomy proposed by Zbigniew Brzezinski in his book *The Grand Chessboard* locates a number of enemy states, including Iran and Iraq as well as China, which must at all costs be prevented from joining their forces. Brzezinski at any rate would not put these three states in the same category as those in the Indian subcontinent. Cooper does not explain how some states remain resolutely modern (and usually badly behaved), whilst others are mired in pre-modernism, or elevated to post-modern status. All live in one world. He will find some explanation for these inequalities if he takes himself to the reports of the United Nations Development Programme in the late years of the last century.

Imperialism or not, these reports show that the combined Gross Domestic Product of forty-eight countries is less than the wealth of the three richest people in the world. Fifteen billionaires have assets greater than the total national income of Africa, south of the Sahara. Thirty-two people own more than the annual income of everyone who lives in South Asia. Eighty-four rich people have holdings greater than the GDP of China, a nation with 1.2 billion citizens.

These inequalities were less yawning when they came to the attention of Tinbergen, who proposed a global plan to diminish them. Basing himself on the best estimates of the means likely to be available in the advanced world, he devised a redistributive plan of aid investment, which took account of the estimated capacities of the underdeveloped countries to deploy it. When his plan was launched, Tinbergen persuaded the United Nations that the aid budgets of the rich countries should be fixed at not less than 0.7% of their GDP. Some years later, I wrote to Tinbergen, who was keenly aware that almost no countries in the rich world had hit his target. He explained to me that the target could not remain static: and that to achieve the same aim of development in the underdeveloped world, it would, in the early 1980s, be necessary to seriously increase the rich world's contribution to the growth of the poor. His calculation was that this would require tripling the input from the economically advanced countries, to 2.1% of GDP. However, rich country aid budgets made no such move: and in fact all shared in a process of attrition, shrinking to pathetic levels. Far from reflecting 'pre-modern' conditions, poor countries show the many faces of poverty, which is every bit as 'modern' or even 'post-modern' as the richer countries which share the same globe. It was the post-modern economy which rewarded the richest 225 persons on the globe with one trillion dollars in 1995, and shared the same sum of money between the poorest 47% of the entire global population. (That is to say, 2.5 billion individuals.) The haves and the have-nots cohabit, and if there is any truth behind the myths of globalisation, the lines which the powerful draw on maps in order to assist the movement of their policemen and soldiers are secondary phenomena, not primary causes. For these, we might enquire at the offices of the IMF or the World Bank.

However, in what Cooper regards as the post-modern world, there has been a degree of transformation in the state system.

Already in the early years of the new Soviet Union, Bertrand Russell had perceived the need for a balancing force to hold the ground between the Russians and the Americans. Hence the political call for a United Europe. Twenty years later, too late to bypass Hitler and the Second World War, Jean Monnet and his colleagues were able to take the first giant steps in this direction, in order to overcome the prolonged conflict between France and Germany.

The establishment of the European Coal and Steel Community pooled the resources of military preparation, and was designed to create an alternative to a renewed arms race between France and Germany. Quite typically, advisors to the British Prime Minister do not choose to emphasise this experiment, which still has residual power and magnetism in the European Union. It has encouraged thoughts about federalism, and developed a working political consensus which until recently remained rather strong, basing itself on the interplay between Social and Christian Democracy. Britain was outside this consensus, and the British establishment loathes it. British participation in the European Union has thus been for the most part reluctant, and apt to call on American support to maintain a pretence of autonomous behaviour. But the development of the European Union has itself been hesitant, and hedged about with difficulties.

Cooper thinks that the peace in Europe is not primarily attributable to responses to the European Union, nor even to Nato. But the European Union was simultaneously an effort to establish pacific co-operation between Europe's main military competitors, and to secure a social balance which could offer an economically workable and electorally viable alternative to Communism, for the great majority of European working populations. The great foreign policy question in all European chancelleries at the end of the Second World War was the 'problem of Germany'. Cooper cuts his teeth in an age when this problem has apparently disappeared: but for a historian with instant recall of the Thirty Years

War this reveals an interestingly patchy amnesia. True, Cooper is interested in the conditions which were propitious for German unity, after the collapse of the Berlin Wall. But the essential, and shaping, initiative which made peace both possible and inevitable in Europe took place fifty years earlier, with the formation of the Coal and Steel Community.

The essential Englishness of Cooper's model is betrayed in one instant flash of perception. 'But if the nation state is a problem then the superstate is certainly not a solution.' This is a reaction against the British travesty of a united Europe, which in truth never sought to create a superstate, but which has always been blackguarded in the British press as a more or less failed attempt to do precisely that.

Federal Europe was an attempt to transcend statehood by opening space for federal democracy. Such space could be assured by varying kinds of confederal relations, and could generate, and hopefully resolve, endless disagreements within the democratic balances that opened up. But it did not constitute a plan for a superstate.

The Christian/Social Democratic social model has been seriously undermined by neo-liberalism during the decade since the end of the Cold War, and its political expression is therefore weakened. The result of the onslaught of liberal reforms, highly satisfactory as it has been to Mrs. Thatcher and Mr. Blair, with his new *entente* embracing Berlusconi and Aznar, has for the time being put paid to Jacques Delors famous promise to the TUC in Britain that Europe was now 'socialism by the backdoor'.

At its height, the European achievement was to hold out a prospect of co-ordinated social development, setting standards which might be extended across the Union. For those who wish to cut back on welfare expenditure it was simple to argue that this betokened an extension of state power. But for the recipients of pensions and welfare support, this was seen as an extension of their human rights, and the state would seem an almost invisible partner. The rules and regulations which were agreed in the heyday of this Europe did not strengthen the state power so much as the principle of individual entitlement. For this reason, there was a great deal of chatter about social Europe, and some progress towards it: but over many years there was scant progress indeed towards the integration of European foreign and security policy.

European convergence has more recently moved into areas which do involve military and diplomatic decision making. These have not served to reinforce popular support for the development of European Union, which has instead been to some extent undermined by the weakening of the social dynamic. Where ten years ago ardent Europeans wished to bring about a standardisation of pension entitlements, and joined us in convening a Pensioners' Parliament, or a European Parliament of Disabled People, now pensioners can happily be left to the mercies of the more parsimonious Member-States, while military policy is supposed to push up to the forefront of the action.

In spite of this, the advance to military Union falters, since parsimony rules there, too. There is no European will to pay for the expensive equipment which would be necessary for the armament of a superstate, especially while neo-liberalism seeks to cull basic social spending.

However, there *is* a superstate, but it is firmly established on the other side of the Atlantic, and it enjoys unparalleled hegemony, with strong economic influence and overwhelming military muscle. The United States of America is the preponderant military power in the modern world, and until this power implodes, it seems set upon flexing its muscles all around the entire globe. Now it asserts itself in Afghanistan, the Philippines, Georgia, Somalia, and Yemen. Tomorrow it is poised to attack Iraq. Iran and North Korea are inscribed on the candidate list for imminent attention. For the time being, however, it is enough for the 'Allies' to be obedient.

Robert Cooper tells us about a gradual breaking down, in Europe, of many of the elements which used to be deemed inseparable from the idea of sovereignty. For sure, he presents us with an idealised picture, but because of the advance of the European idea, this is not completely without reference to reality. However, this picture is achieved by attempting a doctrine of American exceptionalism, since 'it is not clear that the US Government or Congress accepts either the necessity or desirability of interdependence, or its corollaries of openness, mutual surveillance and mutual interference, to the same extent as most European Governments now do'.

This is a prudent admission. The United States confronts and denounces any notion of interdependence. Its openness is for internal consumption, and any surveillance in which it engages is the very opposite of mutual. The United States is number one, and none dare gainsay the fact.

So, the United States defied the International Court of Justice at The Hague, and refused to accept its jurisdiction in the case which was brought by Nicaragua against American piracy, and intimidation. Ever since that time, the United States Government has refused to admit almost all responsibility to international juridical institutions, and has directly rebelled against and rejected the proposals for an International Criminal Court.

In the field of co-ordinated state action, things are no different. The United States has done all it could to wreck the environmental accords of Kyoto, and has shown how skin deep is its commitment to the World Trade Organisation as soon as it began to encounter undesirable implications for American steel policy. Most recently we have seen a series of purges in international organisations, culminating in the dismissal of Ambassador José Bustani, the Brazilian, from the Directorship of the Organisation for the Prohibition of Chemical Weapons.

If the United States can present a terrible punishment to all who threaten its perceived interests, where its own sovereignty is absolute, its view of the sovereignty of others is less dogmatic. Norman Lemann (*New Yorker*, April 1, 2002), in a perceptive account of 'The Next World Order' believes that the Bush Administration may have a 'brand new doctrine of power'.

'I asked Haass [Director of Policy Planning for the State Department] whether there is a doctrine emerging that is as broad as Kennan's containment. "I think there is," he said. "What you are seeing from this Administration is the emergence of a new principle or body of ideas – I'm not sure it constitutes a doctrine – about what you might call the limits of sovereignty. Sovereignty entails obligations. One is not to massacre your own people. Another is not to support terrorism in any way. If a government fails to meet these obligations, then it forfeits some of the normal advantages of sovereignty, including the right to be left alone inside your own territory."'

It is above all in the military field that the United States has staked its claim to be the sole protagonists of the New World Order. The doctrine of Full Spectrum Dominance has now been reiterated across the military community in the United States, in one sententious document after another. 'For the joint force of the future' they tell us in *Joint Vision 2020*, 'Full Spectrum Dominance' [will be achieved, that is] 'the ability of US forces, operating unilaterally or in combination with multinational and interagency partners, to defeat any adversary and control any situation across the full range of military operations'.

Full Spectrum Dominance is not mainly about crushing enemies. Of course, enemies have to be crushed, and the technology has been developed to destroy them utterly. But the political system does not revolve around dead enemies. The major problem is, how to control live allies. Zbigniew Brzezinski summed all this up when he identified the domination of the Eurasian block of states and territories as the necessary first step to global domination. Here are the golden rules:

'The three great imperatives of imperial geostrategy are to prevent collusion and maintain security dependence among the vassals, to keep tributaries pliant and protected and to keep the barbarians from coming together.'

Thus, with the declaration of the unfortunate war on terrorism, Nato rushed to report for duty. Reeling from the shock of the atrocity at the Twin Towers, it was perhaps not surprising that Nato allies instantly agreed to invoke the article in the Nato Treaty which treats an attack on one Member as an attack on all.

With this catch-all declaration of support for the new 'alliance', what did the Americans do? They instantly sidelined Nato altogether from the future action. The war in Afghanistan was not conducted under joint Nato command, but under exclusive American proprietorship. Favoured allies were invited, selectively, to discharge subordinate roles which the Americans deemed appropriate for them. Nato might just as well have not existed, so undeveloped was its joint involvement in the ensuing operations.

If it was perfectly able to ignore an actual alliance, life proved somewhat more difficult in the case of the Arab world, which had been thought to be largely composed of subordinate and compliant states owing fealty to the United States. In fact, the Arab world is in no mood to attack Iraq or even to observe an American attack on that country.

The state system of the Middle East is undoubtedly long past its sell-by date, since it was fashioned out of the collapsing Ottoman Empire by the competing imperialisms of France and England. The advent of the Americans transformed all the dependencies, but resolved none of the inherited problems which arose when the imperial powers drew lines across the map, and fashioned protectorates according to what caprice they fancied.

The large Kurdish population in that post-First World War settlement had no state, but was dispersed across several. Yet another full-scale war against Iraq would be bound to reawaken Kurdish discontent with this unsustainable situation. But the victims of this discontent would include many former allies of the United States, who would find the resultant chaos painful to bear. In the same way, all the fractures in the Muslim world, all the ancient grievances of Sunnis and Shiites, would be forcefully recalled.

All this implies that unchallenged military power is no golden key to the future. Although they can vaporise the entire Middle East, the Americans are in grave danger of losing any vestige of influence over it.

This just makes matters worse. The more insecure they feel, the more the Americans look for security in weapons. Now it becomes necessary to jump the barriers and go nuclear.

The January 2002 United States Nuclear Posture Review reaffirms the centrality of nuclear weapons in US national security policy. Its basic thrust is to attain maximum flexibility with regard to nuclear arsenal size and capabilities, with minimum treaty limitations. Essentially, the Review relocates nuclear weapons within a broad spectrum of warfighting capabilities. The review fundamentally contradicts US commitments and obligations to non-nuclear signatories of the Nuclear Non-Proliferation Treaty (NPT). It also calls into question the commitments under the NPT of the six European Nato members, including the United Kingdom, who share in the use of United States nuclear weapons based in Europe.

Does this mean, then, that we should follow Robert Cooper in his elaborate model of post-modern imperialism? Not if Occam's razor still exists.

The simple map of the modern political world charts American power and its influences. If there are derelict areas in which 'pre-modern' rules apply, that is because the United States had found no use for their resources, and no strategic advantage from bombing them or exacting tribute from them.

Many strategic uses have been propounded for contested areas such as Afghanistan, most of them involving resources, whether oil or water. But the initial attraction of Afghanistan for the United States was almost purely geo-strategic, since the Soviet influence over Afghanistan and subsequent invasion of that country provided a golden opportunity to humiliate the Soviets, and 'avenge the Vietnam war'. This, indeed, was Brzezinski's stated reason for investing so much effort in the Afghanistan mountains. This was also the reason for inventing and honing the lawless legions of Osama bin Laden, who was patented in the United States and designed to bring tribulation to its enemies.

Indeed, was not Saddam Hussein also a creature of the United States and its most intimate allies, when he was encouraged eastwards into war with Iran? The war against terrorism is largely designed to liquidate the unforeseen consequences of American policy on terrorism, always capricious, never influenced by conscience, and ever likely to go wrong.

Precisely because Europe is in a ghostly 'post-modern' state, it is not a state, and is acutely ill-designed to pretend to be an imperial power. Cooper thinks that membership of the Union may create some sort of analogue to the British Commonwealth. But unless the rules of the Union are changed, membership entails rights and duties, the so-called *acquis communitaire*.

Already, the attempts at enlargement are deeply troubled by this problem, because free movement of capital, without concomitant free movement of labour, will create powerful tension in the old Community heartland. The more that the constitution of the European Union is tampered with and subverted, to the disadvantage of consistency and principled action, the greater the jeopardy in which the Union will find itself. Freedom of movement of capital, but not of labour, may solve some diplomatic problems with the Poles, but the problems which it will create will not be simply diplomatic, but will engender real economic conflicts. How could this problem be overcome by creating client states for Europe's Member-States? The idea is unlikely because it will constitute a complete reversion to what Cooper thinks of as imperialism, abandoning all the virtues which he associates with post-modernism. Much though the Emperor Blair might relish the opportunity to wear funny hats around his part of Afghanistan, any more fundamental economic relationship will prove impossible to fix, because the conquest of territories is liable to settle on the rule of a single power. What to share with others? The benefits or the bills? The European Union as a collective imperial power would be in no better case: a permanent quarrel between the Member-States, in which the colonies would always be free to play their Lords and Masters off against one another. This invention won't run.

Robert Cooper's elaborate picture of the preconditions for a new kind of 'benign' imperialism will not persuade any of the victims, and will rapidly prove impractical for those who might temporarily lay claim to this or that piece of empire. He is drawn into the attempt to theorise all this out of the chaos which has been generated by Full Spectrum Dominance. Full Spectrum Dominance is the residual half of the Cold War couplet, founded on an incredible arms race, and able to build monstrously swollen military machines. The Russian half of this competition collapsed because the Soviet economy was too feeble to sustain it. The Americans have commanded larger resources, but their half of this military monster is surely also likely to implode.

Security will surely be difficult to find in the only place in which it can reside, which is, Full Spectrum Democracy. Had we been wiser, we might have been able to state the case for Full Spectrum Democracy before the end of the Cold War, and to create a basis for the approach to it. Now we are compelled to suffer from our oversights during those days, and there will be more fraught and perilous times as the domination syndrome continues to work its way through the political system. Yes, this could kill us all, since there are those with great power and influence in the United States who are concerned to make their most efficacious weapons more effective by giving them a nuclear bite.

But this map of power which is grandly and boastfully charted by Mr. Blair's advisers, is a map of the road to nowhere. Only by setting ourselves the agenda of Full Spectrum Democracy, by asking what it entails and bringing its goals within our sights, will we ever become able to visualise a world in which our children will find it fit to live.

Removing Refugee Protection

The hidden cost of September 11th

Liz Fekete

Liz Fekete is head of European research at the Institute of Race Relations (www.irr.org.uk) where she edits the European Race Bulletin. This article forms part of a special issue of the Bulletin entitled Racism: the hidden cost of September 11, which is available from the Institute.

The emergency powers and other policing measures adopted by European Union member states amid one-dimensional parliamentary and media debate, are generating a climate and culture of suspicion across Europe against foreigners, with Arabs, asylum seekers and those of Middle-Eastern appearance emerging as the new 'enemy aliens'. It is a 'sus' culture which has been given respectability by the EU's attempts to abandon international laws which, first, guarantee asylum rights to those involved in legitimate acts of political violence in their home countries (on the grounds that rebellion is sometimes necessary to overthrow repression) and, second, grant protection to those foreign nationals who are, by international law, 'non-removable' because they cannot be sent back to countries that practise torture or capital punishment. It is a 'sus' culture, that, in demonising asylum seekers as terrorists, leads to the lowering of standards of refugee protection by increasing possibilities for exclusion. While this power to exclude is not entirely new (the Refugee Convention itself provides that protection should not be given to those reasonably believed to be guilty of 'war crimes, crimes against humanity, acts contrary to the purposes and principles of the UN, or serious non-political crimes, committed outside the country of origin'), its extent and scope is no longer clearly limited and defined. And this power to exclude has, of course, been further legitimised by the EU Council's attack on refugees' right to oppose tyranny abroad (as evidenced in the failure of EU law to distinguish between terrorism and legitimate political violence).

The following cases illustrate the ways in which the standards of refugee protection have been lowered, and a climate of suspicion has been ratcheted up since September 11.

Zari and Ahmed Hussein Agaiza, who have lived in Sweden since 1999 and whose asylum applications are still pending, were forcibly returned to Egypt on 18 December 2001 on an Egyptian government aeroplane. Agaiza had been sentenced in absentia in Egypt to 25 years hard labour on charges of taking part in an armed attack on the Egyptian embassy in Pakistan – charges which he denies, saying that he was living in Iran at the time of the bomb attack. The Swedish authorities recognised that the men had a well-founded fear of persecution but still excluded them from protection on the basis of connections to organisations which had been responsible for acts of terrorism.

In October 2001, Muhammad Abd Rahman Bilasi-Ashri, an Egyptian asylum seeker sentenced in absentia to 15 years in prison for supporting Egyptian Islamic Jihad, was arrested in Austria. A court quickly ordered his extradition, even though in 1999 the Supreme Court had ruled against his extradition. Bilasi-Ashri's name surfaced during a British investigation of London-based Islamic radicals suspected of involvement in the bombings of two US embassies in Africa in 1998, according to a British police memo. But the British inquiry on him has been dropped.

A Kurdish woman, Nuriye Kesbir, who is a member of the Kurdistan Workers Party (PKK) presidential council in Turkey, has been in detention in the Netherlands since her arrival on 27 September 2001 and faces extradition despite her asylum claim and despite the likelihood of torture (rape and sexual humiliation of women prisoners in Turkey is well documented) and the death penalty. The PKK is not banned in the Netherlands.

Mohamed Chalabi had already served an eight-year prison sentence in France for his role as head of a support network of the Group of Armed Islam (GIA). As he was born in France, and is the father of four French children, he should have been protected from deportation to Algeria. Moreover, normally such prisoners, having served their sentence in France, would be deported to a safe third country rather than being sent to a country where they would face the death penalty. Nevertheless, on 9 November 2001, the French government acceded to an Algerian request and returned Chalabi to Algeria.

Zakaria Toukal, despite support from the computer company which employs him, could be deported to Algeria. Toukal, who spent eleven months in custody awaiting trial, was originally picked up for questioning in the course of an inquiry into the Chalabi network. Subsequently released, but still awaiting the court case, Toukal married a French student, fathered two children, completed a degree course in robotics and gained employment as a research and development engineer. Then, in March 2000, Toukal was convicted, but the instruction that he be permanently removed from France was not enacted and he continued to live and work legally in France, with his residence permit regularly renewed. But after September 11, the authorities – concerned about his robotics degree – arrested him and placed him under administrative detention. A first attempt to deport him to Algeria failed when he refused to board the plane. An appeal has been launched and Toukal has asked the interior minister to place him under house arrest with the right to work. The Alcatel company has kept his job open for him.

In Germany, a new law has been introduced to allow the state to disband religious organisations with suspected links to terrorism. At the same time, the government is negotiating with Turkey for the extradition of the radical Islamist Metin Kaplan, who heads the Cologne-based Islamic group, the 'Caliphate State', and is wanted in Turkey on treason charges. Previously, Germany had resisted the extradition of Kaplan, who has been imprisoned in Germany since 1999 on public order charges, on the grounds that Kaplan would be subjected to torture and the death penalty. But now it is pressing ahead with extradition.

From demonisation to exclusion

The background to these exclusions predates September 11. Indeed, for several years, there has been pressure on European governments from countries such as Turkey, Saudi Arabia, Algeria and Sri Lanka, to alter asylum policies so as to make extradition of political dissidents easier. The allegation, repeated over and over again, was that Europe's asylum system provided a safe haven for terrorists, thereby allowing terrorist organisations to regroup in Europe and exploit it as an organisational and logistical base from which to raise funds, procure arms and plot terrorist attacks in their country of origin. Many European countries had attempted to appease their overseas critics with whom they had military, diplomatic and economic ties. But, prior to September 11, this did not so much involve caving in to extradition requests as institutionalising the 'dissident=terrorist' equation through anti-terrorist laws which proscribed various political parties and associated social organisations and created new offences based on association with proscribed organisations, rather than on actual involvement in illegitimate violence.

But since September 11, while there has been further pressure towards proscription, the most significant development has been the increasing willingness to acquiesce to extradition requests, to appease not just international partners in the Coalition Against Terrorism but also the UN Security Council. Previously, extradition requests from countries that practised torture were refused, on the grounds that refugees and asylum seekers were protected under international treaties, European law and the tradition that the threat of torture overrides any extradition requests. But, in September 2001, in the first clear prompt to change existing practice, the UN Security Council passed a resolution urging that states 'ensure in conformity with international law, that refugee status is not abused by the perpetrators, organisers or facilitators of terrorist acts, and that claims of political motivation are not recognised as grounds for refusing requests for the extradition of alleged terrorists'. Then, on October 16, president Bush wrote to Romano Prodi, president of the European Commission, suggesting 40 measures to combat terrorism, including a request to bypass the extradition process and 'explore alternatives to extradition including expulsion and deportation'. This was followed by the publication of an EU working document in December that suggested that, in future, it would be legitimate to extradite people to states that practise torture, as long as 'legal guarantees' were received from that state that no such torture would be practised. Ominously, the EU working document stated that after September 11, the European Court of Human Rights may need to rule again on the balance 'between the protection needs of the individual set off against the security interests of the state'.

It is this pressure, principally from the UN Security Council and the US, then, that provides the background to the cases outlined above – cases that are viewed by civil libertarians across Europe as constituting human rights abuses carried out by European governments. Many human rights organisations in Europe have alerted the public to the degradation of democracy and human rights standards that such secret and sickening deals incur. Thus, the League of Human Rights described the secret deal between the French ministry of foreign affairs and the Algerian government to deport Mohamed Chalabi as a 'sordid procedure' amounting to 'extradition in disguise', only made possible in the post-September 11 climate. In Austria, lawyers for the Egyptian facing trial at home for Islamic activism, have condemned the government's decision to extradite as nothing more than 'revenge for September 11'. The Swedish branch of Amnesty International (AI) has described the proceedings surrounding the deportation of the two Egyptian asylum seekers who the Swedish Security Police (Säpo) accused of being members of an armed Islamist group, as grossly unfair. It accuses the Swedish government of being in breach of its international obligations not to send anyone back to a country where he or she would be at risk of serious human rights violations. Another case, involving four Islamists arrested on the information of a tortured al-Qaida suspect in Algeria (information he later retracted) is causing consternation in the Netherlands. Yet, politicians seem impervious to criticism. In Germany, the federal interior minister responsible for new anti-terrorist legislation, has promised that the new laws will make deportations such as that of Metlin Kaplan easier and the Right's candidate in the 2002 presidential elections, Edmund Stoiber, only agreed to back anti-terrorist legislation on condition that more such deportations followed.

Partners with state terror

Governments justify extradition on the grounds that they have, or will receive, guarantees that those sent back will not be tortured or subjected to the death penalty. But Amnesty has pointed out that such guarantees are an 'insufficient safeguard', as acknowledged by the European Court of Human Rights which, in 1996, told the British government to refuse an extradition request from the government of India for a Sikh resident in Britain on the ground that written guarantees of proper treatment could not facilitate extradition because whatever the 'good faith of the Indian government', the violation of human rights 'is a recalcitrant and enduring problem in India'. Amnesty has already documented evidence that Ahmed Hussein Agaiza, extradited from Sweden to Egypt, has been held in isolation, tortured and now has difficulty in moving. And although Algeria guaranteed not to imprison Chalabi, he was immediately arrested on arrival in Algiers and charged with 'creating and belonging to an armed terrorist group which had intended to commit crimes of devastation and destruction'. Such facts do not seem to concern politicians unduly. Germany's interior minister, Otto Schily, says that he would be happy to return suspects to such countries as Egypt, Algeria and Turkey as long as he can get guarantees that they will not face the death penalty.

In fact, what these cases demonstrate is Europe's increasing links with authoritarian regimes that practise state terror, something that has long concerned human rights organisations and lawyers who have been exposing the close working relationship between European security services and secret services abroad involved in widespread human rights abuses. For example, Germany, which proscribed the PKK in 1993 and Kurdish associations believed to finance the PKK, has had a close working relationship with Turkey while France has worked with the Algerian government to target Islamic fundamentalists living in France. The UK's Terrorism Act 2000, with its list of proscribed organisations, undoubtedly reflected the close working relationship the British secret services were developing with their counterparts in countries like Sri Lanka, Turkey and Algeria.

But since September 11, these informal relationships are being institutionalised at the highest level, thanks to the imperatives of the International Coalition Against Terrorism. The deals being struck, the information exchanged, go well beyond the fight against al-Qaeda. The US and Europe are launching a 'War Against Terrorism' which has in its sights a myriad of organisations and political movements across the globe, which are not connected to al-Qaeda and cannot be understood simply as 'religious jihads'. Rather, they require a contextual understanding of the concrete political and social problems of their countries. The War Against Terrorism is leading European governments to embrace those countries that, in practising state terror, create the very culture of repression which drives oppositional groups towards rebellion and may lead them to respond to terror with terror tactics of their own. A European-wide approach to the anti-terrorist fight, which would have examined cause and effect in particular countries and adopted specific policies accordingly, has been thrown out in favour of the instant gratification of immediate arrests for the benefit of appeasing coalition partners, particularly the US.

Preparing the Unthinkable

The United States Nuclear Posture Review

William Arkin

William M. Arkin is a senior fellow at the Johns Hopkins University School of Advanced International Studies in Washington and an adjunct professor at the US Air Force School of Advanced Airpower Studies. He is also a consultant to a number of non-governmental organisations and a regular contributor to the Bulletin of the Atomic Scientists.

The Bush administration, in a secret policy review completed early this year, has ordered the Pentagon to draft contingency plans for the use of nuclear weapons against at least seven countries, naming not only Russia and the 'axis of evil' – Iraq, Iran, and North Korea – but also China, Libya and Syria.

In addition, the United States Defence Department has been told to prepare for the possibility that nuclear weapons may be required in some future Arab-Israeli crisis. And, it is to develop plans for using nuclear weapons to retaliate against chemical or biological attacks, as well as 'surprising military developments' of an unspecified nature.

These and a host of other directives, including calls for developing bunker-busting mini-nukes and nuclear weapons that reduce collateral damage, are contained in a still-classified document called the Nuclear Posture Review (NPR), which was delivered to Congress on January 8. Like all such documents since the dawning of the Atomic Age more than a half-century ago, this Review offers a chilling glimpse into the world of nuclear-war planners: with a Strangelovian genius, they cover every conceivable circumstance in which a president might wish to use nuclear weapons – planning in great detail for a war they hope never to wage.

In this top-secret domain, there has always been an inconsistency between America's diplomatic objectives of reducing nuclear arsenals and preventing the proliferation of weapons of mass destruction, on the one hand, and the military imperative to prepare for the unthinkable, on the other.

Nevertheless, the Bush administration plan reverses an almost two-decades-long trend of relegating nuclear weapons to the category of weapons of last resort. It also redefines nuclear requirements in hurried post-September 11 terms. In these and other ways, the still-secret document offers insights into the evolving views of nuclear strategists in Secretary Donald H. Rumsfeld's Defence Department.

While downgrading the threat from Russia and publicly emphasising their commitment to reducing the number of long-range nuclear weapons, Defence Department strategists promote tactical and so-called 'adaptive' nuclear capabilities to deal with contingencies where large nuclear arsenals are not demanded. They seek a host of new weapons and support systems, including conventional military and cyber warfare capabilities integrated with nuclear warfare. The end product is a now-familiar post-Afghanistan model – with nuclear capability added. It combines precision weapons, long-range strikes, and special and covert operations.

But the Review's call for development of new nuclear weapons that reduce 'collateral damage' myopically ignores the political, moral and military implications – short-term and long – of crossing the nuclear threshold. Under what circumstances might nuclear weapons be used under the new posture? The Review says they 'could be employed against targets able to withstand non-nuclear attack,' or in retaliation for the use of nuclear, biological, or chemical weapons, or 'in the event of surprising military developments.' Planning nuclear-strike capabilities, it says, involves the recognition of 'immediate, potential or unexpected' contingencies. North Korea, Iraq, Iran, Syria and Libya are named as 'countries that could be involved' in all three kinds of threat. 'All have long-standing hostility towards the United States and its security partners. All sponsor or harbour terrorists, and have active weapons of mass destruction and missile programmes.'

China, because of its nuclear forces and 'developing strategic objectives,' is listed as 'a country that could be involved in an immediate or potential contingency.' Specifically, the Review lists a military confrontation over the status of Taiwan as one of the scenarios that could lead Washington to use nuclear weapons. Other listed scenarios for nuclear conflict are a North Korean attack on South Korea and an Iraqi assault on Israel or its neighbours.

The second important insight the Review offers into Pentagon thinking about nuclear policy is the extent to which the Bush administration's strategic planners were shaken by last September's terrorist attacks on the World Trade Centre and the Pentagon. Though Congress directed the new administration 'to conduct a comprehensive review of US nuclear forces' before the events of September 11, the final study is striking for its single-minded reaction to those tragedies.

Heretofore, nuclear strategy tended to exist as something apart from the ordinary challenges of foreign policy and military affairs. Nuclear weapons were not just the option of last resort, they were the option reserved for times when national survival hung in the balance – a doomsday confrontation with the Soviet Union, for instance.

Now, nuclear strategy seems to be viewed through the prism of September 11. For one thing, the Bush administration's faith in old-fashioned deterrence is gone. It no longer takes a superpower to pose a dire threat to Americans. 'The terrorists who struck us on September 11th were clearly not deterred from doing so by the massive US nuclear arsenal,' Rumsfeld told an audience at the National Defence University in late January. Similarly, US Under-secretary of State John R. Bolton said in a recent interview, 'We would do whatever is necessary to defend America's innocent civilian population .... The idea that fine theories of deterrence work against everybody ... has just been disproven by Sept. 11.'

Moreover, while insisting they would go nuclear only if other options seemed inadequate, officials are looking for nuclear weapons that could play a role in the kinds of challenges the United States faces with al Qaeda. Accordingly, the Review calls for new emphasis on developing such things as nuclear bunker-busters and surgical 'warheads that reduce collateral damage,' as well as weapons that could be used against smaller, more circumscribed targets – 'possible modifications to existing weapons to provide additional yield flexibility,' in the jargon-rich language of the Review. It also proposes to train US Special Forces operators to play the same intelligence gathering and targeting roles for nuclear weapons that they now play for conventional weapons strikes in Afghanistan. And cyber-warfare and other non-nuclear military capabilities would be integrated into nuclear-strike forces to make them more all-encompassing.

As for Russia, once the primary reason for having a US nuclear strategy, the review says that while Moscow's nuclear programmes remain cause for concern, 'ideological sources of conflict' have been eliminated, rendering a nuclear contingency involving Russia 'plausible' but 'not expected'. 'In the event that US relations with Russia significantly worsen in the future,' the Review says, 'the US may need to revise its nuclear force levels and posture.'

When completion of the Review was publicly announced in January, Pentagon briefers deflected questions about most of the specifics, saying the information was classified. Officials did stress that, consistent with a Bush campaign pledge, the plan called for reducing the current 6,000 long-range nuclear weapons to one-third that number over the next decade. Rumsfeld, who approved the Review late last year, said the administration was seeking 'a new approach to strategic deterrence', to include missile defences and improvements in non-nuclear capabilities. Also, Russia would no longer be officially defined as 'an enemy'. Beyond that, almost no details were revealed.

The classified text, however, is shot through with a world view transformed by September 11. The Review coins the phrase 'New Triad', which it describes as comprising the 'offensive strike leg', (nuclear and conventional forces) plus 'active and passive defences', (anti- missile systems and other defences) and 'a responsive defence infrastructure' (the ability to develop and produce nuclear weapons and resume nuclear testing). Previously, the nuclear 'triad' was the bombers, long-range land-based missiles and submarine-launched missiles that formed the three legs of America's strategic arsenal.

The Review emphasises the integration of 'new non-nuclear strategic capabilities' into nuclear-war plans. 'New capabilities must be developed to defeat emerging threats such as hard and deeply-buried targets (HDBT), to find and attack mobile and re-locatable targets, to defeat chemical and biological agents, and to improve accuracy and limit collateral damage,' the Review says. It calls for 'a new strike system' using four converted Trident submarines, an unmanned combat air vehicle and a new air-launched cruise missile as potential new weapons.

Beyond new nuclear weapons, the review proposes establishing what it calls an 'agent defeat' programme, which defence officials say includes a 'boutique' approach to finding new ways of destroying deadly chemical or biological warfare agents, as well as penetrating enemy facilities that are otherwise difficult to attack. This includes, according to the document, 'thermal, chemical or radiological neutralisation of chemical/biological materials in production or storage facilities.' Bush administration officials stress that the development and integration of non-nuclear capabilities into the nuclear force is what permits reductions in traditional long-range weaponry. But the blueprint laid down in the Review would expand the breadth and flexibility of US nuclear capabilities.

In addition to the new weapons systems, the review calls for incorporation of 'nuclear capability' into many of the conventional systems now under development. An extended-range conventional cruise missile in the works for the US Air Force 'would have to be modified to carry nuclear warheads if necessary. Similarly, the F-35 Joint Strike Fighter should be modified to carry nuclear weapons 'at an affordable price'. The Review calls for research to begin on fitting an existing nuclear warhead to a new 5,000-pound 'earth penetrating' munition.

Given the advances in electronics and information technologies in the past decade, it is not surprising that the Review also stresses improved satellites and intelligence, communications, and more robust high-bandwidth decision-making systems. Particularly noticeable is the directive to improve US capabilities in the field of 'information operations', or cyber- warfare. The intelligence community 'lacks adequate data on most adversary computer local area networks and other command and control systems', the Review observes. It calls for improvements in the ability to 'exploit' enemy computer networks, and the integration of cyber-warfare into the overall nuclear war database 'to enable more effective targeting, weaponeering, and combat assessment essential to the New Triad'.

In recent months, when Bush administration officials talked about the implications of September 11 for long-term military policy, they have often focused on 'homeland defence' and the need for an anti-missile shield. In truth, what has evolved since last year's terror attacks is an integrated, significantly expanded planning doctrine for nuclear wars.

Purging the International Community

A Dossier

The Case of José Bustani

José Bustani was elected the first Director-General of the Organisation for the Prohibition of Chemical Weapons by acclamation on 13 May 1997, and was re-appointed for a second four-year term of office commencing in May 2001 by an unprecedented unanimous decision of the Conference of the States Parties in May 2000.

José Bustani, the distinguished Director-General of the Organisation for the Prohibition of Chemical Weapons, was dismissed from his post on 23 April 2002. This followed a sustained campaign for his removal by the United States government. Mr Bustani explains the worrying implications of his removal for the proper conduct of international organisations in this, his statement to the Conference of the States Parties to the Chemical Weapons Convention which met in The Hague.

The Organisation for the Prohibition of Chemical Weapons came into existence on 29 April 1997. Its deed of foundation—the Chemical Weapons Convention—aims to achieve four principal objectives: the elimination of chemical weapons and of the capacity to develop them, the verification of non-proliferation, international assistance and protection in the event of the use or threat of use of chemical weapons, and international co-operation and assistance in the peaceful use of chemistry.

*   *   *   *

Back in 1997, when I decided to accept the request of the Brazilian Government to submit my candidature for the position of Director-General of the Organisation for the Prohibition of Chemical Weapons, I considered it, and I still consider it, an honour to be granted the unique opportunity to contribute to the first *ever truly* global attempt to abolish an entire category of weapons of mass destruction. But more than anything, I decided to run for the post of Director-General because the Chemical Weapons Convention represents the international community's biggest ever achievement in the area of disarmament and non-proliferation. It is the first – and only – truly non-discriminatory multilateral disarmament treaty in existence – it is a treaty which places equal responsibilities on, and gives equal rights to, all States Parties.

Countries possessing chemical weapons that embraced the Chemical Weapons Convention have been divesting themselves of those travesties of history because they are assured that stockpiles of those weapons existing elsewhere are also being destroyed, under a stringent verification regime. The Convention establishes no special treatment for countries with a large chemical industry. Developing countries, when they declare themselves ready to enhance international security by joining the Organisation, have, in their vast majority, little understanding of chemical weapons; yet, they immediately see the benefit in participating, through the greater access to technology and technical assistance to which they become entitled. Indeed, the Convention declares itself to be in favour of the broadest possible co-operation among States Parties in respect of peaceful uses of chemistry. Furthermore, the Convention requires us all to make every effort to extend its regime universally – with no exceptions. As a result, during my first five years as Director-General, no Member State was considered 'more equal' than others. And I have never subscribed to the theory that 'equality' is proportional to the size of any one state's budgetary contribution.

Those were the promises inherent in the Convention – as I saw them at the time, and as I continue to see them today. That was the basis of the 'vision' that I brought to the Organisation on my very first day in the job. That was the vision that was amply clear to all, and not challenged by anyone, when my term was extended by acclamation in May 2000, one year ahead of schedule. That was the vision that I vowed to uphold back in 1997, and that is the vision that I intend to keep intact as long as I remain Director-General. Yet – if I am to believe the various allegations of my 'ill-conceived initiatives' – that vision is now being rejected by some members of this Organisation.

Of course I was always aware that the job of Director-General of the Organisation for the Prohibition of Chemical Weapons would not be an easy one. I knew that I was going to face considerable pressures, and that my integrity might be put to the test. I realised that immediately after I was elected Director-General, when I had to fight in order to put together a team of trusted colleagues, on the basis of their competence and ability, and not of the political pressures brought to bear upon me. I realised this again shortly thereafter, when one Member State tried – unsuccessfully – to force me to provide it with copies of each and every inspection report. I realise it even more deeply now, when one Member State is leading the campaign for my immediate departure from the Organisation for the Prohibition of Chemical Weapons, allegedly because of my 'management style'. Yet, I am as convinced now as I was then, that the Chemical Weapons Convention will survive only if the principles of *genuine* multilateralism, true fairness, and equal treatment are preserved. And those are the principles that I have been trying to uphold every day of the last five years.

I am truly proud of the Organisation's achievements in those five years. I am proud of the staff of the Secretariat. Member States should be grateful to every one of those 500 hard-working professionals for what the Organisation for the Prohibition of Chemical Weapons has been able to accomplish. I am proud of the unprecedented growth in the membership of the Organisation – which is the clearest evidence of the respect for the Organisation for the Prohibition of Chemical Weapons amongst its States Parties, as well as amongst the ever-dwindling number of States not party. I am proud that we have established a sound and impartial verification regime, and that we are fortunate to have inspectors who have placed impartiality, decency, and ethics above everything. Their loyalty is to the Organisation, and not to individual Member States. I am proud of the more than 1,100 inspections we have conducted in more than 50 Member States; and of the non-discriminatory and unbiased way in which we conducted them. I am proud of the proposal which is now before the Executive Council for the provision of effective and timely assistance to victims of chemical weapons attacks, including attacks by terrorists. And I am proud of the modest, yet extremely significant, effort we put into our international co-operation programmes, which, I firmly believe, are critical to the struggle against the proliferation of chemical weapons. I have faith that the Organisation will ultimately succeed in its mission to completely destroy the world's chemical weapons arsenals. As I have stated before, once its disarmament mission has been accomplished, the Organisation for the Prohibition of Chemical Weapons should become an 'organisation for the promotion of chemistry for peaceful purposes', in full accordance with the spirit of the Convention.

Against the backdrop of these achievements, I can only see the attack launched against me as an attack on the Organisation itself, and, in particular, on those key principles which have been guiding my work, and which have become the hallmark of my 'management style'. Indeed, the unprecedented effort that has been put into ensuring my dismissal suggests the intention to change much more at the Organisation for the Prohibition of Chemical Weapons than the personality of its Director-General, or his 'management style'. And this would explain why my appeals for dialogue and co-operation have been repeatedly rejected. Contrary to the path of stonewalling and hostility which my critics have chosen, I still believe that dialogue and co-operation offer the best way out of any crisis, including the current one, for the benefit of the Convention and all States Parties. Let me repeat again that, even at this very late stage, and in spite of the many slanderous remarks that have been made about me in the course of the last few months, I still stand ready and willing to follow the path of dialogue and co-operation.

No one can disregard the fact that the Organisation for the Prevention of Chemical Weapons works, and works well. And it has the respect and support of the vast majority of its 145 States Parties. The Organisation has become too strong to be destroyed from the outside. This may explain the current attempt to implode it from within, together with its underlying principles of fairness and non-discrimination. The culture of non-discrimination and equal treatment that I have fought hard to establish in the Secretariat is now under attack. That culture is being challenged by one of silent and unquestioning obedience to one or a few 'major contributors'. If this 'new culture' is to prevail, then those members of staff who act with integrity and are committed to fairness will have to be the first to go – starting with the Director-General.

Those of you who have been closely following the work of the Organisation certainly realise what it is about my management style that appears to be causing discomfort in some quarters. I could have been just a figurehead, as some Member States wanted. Instead I have chosen, as the Convention requires, to take my responsibilities seriously, amongst other things by being actively involved in the everyday work of the Organisation. I refused to defer to those individuals who some Member States want to be in charge.

Ironically enough, because I have stood in the way of decisions that would have established a double standard in the Organisation, I am now accused of being biased. What is bias for some, is in reality my commitment to 'equal treatment for all'. I insist that the scope of access for our inspectors should be the same in all countries. I also insist that States Parties cannot pick and choose those areas which inspectors may or may not verify. I insist that the verification effort, in full accordance with the Convention, should be aimed at inspectable facilities, rather than at certain countries. I insist on measures that will ensure that Organisation inspectors verify those weapons and equipment which the Organisation must verify, rather than merely those which might be volunteered by a State Party for verification. In other words, *I trust, but I also verify, everywhere*, in full accordance with the Convention. I do criticise attempts to water down the verification regime. I do criticise the continuing attempts of a small number of States Parties to stonewall long-awaited solutions to critical issues out of perceived national preferences. And I am now facing this current ongoing ordeal because I should not, perhaps, have drawn the attention of other Member States to these matters, as the Convention requires.

What else about my management style is not liked that might require changing? Let us examine the list of my 'ill-conceived initiatives'.

I am blamed for seeking Iraq's membership of the Chemical Weapons Convention, even though this effort is in full accordance with the decisions of the United Nations Security Council, and with the mandate issued to me by all of you, to ensure the Convention's universality *without exception*. Does dissatisfaction with my actions mean that the universality of the Convention should include some countries, but not others, not Iraq, for example?

I am blamed for seeking to establish, in full accordance with Article X of the Convention, a credible system to protect States Parties from an attack, including a terrorist attack, with chemical weapons. Should as many as two-thirds of Member States remain defenceless against such a threat, while the ability of a small number of other States to protect themselves and their allies remains robust?

I am blamed for holding out the Organisation's hand to the international community in its fight against terrorism, simply because the Organisation has unique expertise in chemical weapons to offer in this regard. Is that a crime? Or is it a compassionate and rational offer, on the basis of my assessment of the very real contribution which the Organisation for the Prohibition of Chemical

Weapons, in close consultation with other international organisations, will have to make in the post September 11th context?

I am now reproached for fully funding in 2001 one single international co-operation programme which amounted to just 0.4 percent of the Organisation budget for that year, yet which meant a great deal to the many developing countries. This programme represents the vital link between disarmament and development that has been recognised and endorsed by the United Nations. Do Member States seek to further reduce the international co-operation and assistance programmes at the Organisation for the Prohibition of Chemical Weapons, which at present account for a meagre 6% of its budget?

Finally, I am blamed for wishing to keep all States Parties informed of progress in the destruction of Russia's chemical weapons, and for suggesting that Russia's utilisation of international assistance be scrutinised by the international community. If those are my ill-conceived initiatives, then I plead guilty as charged.

I believe that any abandonment of such sound policies will have extremely serious consequences for the Organisation and for you, the Member States. This is why I insisted that my fate should be decided by all of you, the States Parties, and not by one, or a few 'major contributors', which, in supporting the United States draft decision, appear to share the United States perception of my 'errors of judgement'.

I will be frank – a major blow is being struck against the Organisation for the Prohibition of Chemical Weapons. And the perpetrators would have preferred it to take place behind closed doors. They were absolutely confident that they could move any piece on the global chessboard *ad libitum*, without consultation or explanation to the rest of the world and, in particular, to the rest of the Organisation's membership. This is why, in flagrant violation of the letter, not to mention the spirit, of the Chemical Weapons Convention, the Brazilian Government was unilaterally approached with the demand that I resign and be 'reassigned'. Much later, I was approached unilaterally with ultimatums to step down. And the campaign did not stop, even when a clear majority of the 41 members of the Executive Council declined to support the United States 'no-confidence motion' requesting me to stand down.

As I wrote to your Foreign Ministers, there is a more important and fundamental point to consider. Much more than the person of the Director-General – and, please, forget Jose Bustani now – or even the Organisation for the Prohibition of Chemical Weapons itself, is at stake here. No Director-General, of any international organisation in history, has ever been dismissed during his or her term of office. Moreover, no Director-General should be dismissed without due process, without any evidence of malfeasance being produced by the accuser, and without, at the very least, an open discussion and an independent investigation of the allegations. Those of you who have been following developments at the Organisation for the Prohibition of Chemical Weapons know that I have committed no crime. You know that the so-called allegations against me are trumped up charges. You know that there is no mismanagement of the Organisation's budget, and that every cent has been spent on activities that were properly budgeted for. The latest report by the External Auditor – on the 2001 financial year – is the clearest possible indication of this. It will be formally issued in the next few days, but has already given us a perfectly clean bill of health, once again, for 2001. You know that my offer of a full and independent inquiry into my performance as the Director-General was rejected because such an inquiry would simply expose the allegations as absolutely unfounded, and confirm that there has never been any wrongdoing. The United States draft decision, in fact, establishes a precedent whereby the Director-General or Secretary-General of any international organisation can be removed from office at any time during his or her tenure, simply because one Member State, with or without other 'major contributors', doesn't like his or her 'management style', or has 'lost confidence' in him or her, whatever this might mean. And to establish such a precedent within an organisation such as the Organisation for the Prohibition of Chemical Weapons, which is not in the public eye of the international community as are some of its cousins, is easy. This is what this Conference is about. These are the choices you face.

Now let me say a few words to those who are concerned about the Organisation for the Prohibition of Chemical Weapon's survival, should one very important Member State not pay its budgetary contribution to the Organisation. I fundamentally disagree with those who may think that it is better to surrender the Organisation to that Member State, than to maintain a truly multilateral Organisation at minimal additional cost. I will never agree that the façade of multilateralism is more important than its substance. This would not be a compromise – it would be capitulation. Why? I will explain. This Member State's contribution to this year's budget is 12 million euros, six million of which have already been paid. Is six million euros too high a price to pay for ensuring the independence and effectiveness of the Organisation? Is six million euros (or even 10 or 12 million euros, should other like-minded Member States also refuse to pay their dues) too high a price to pay to avoid ousting the sitting head of an international organisation, something never yet attempted in international law? Is the Organisation for the Prohibition of Chemical Weapon's independence this cheap?

Now, let me say a few words about the immediate future. Those who believe that, if I leave, the Organisation will be flooded with money, are sadly mistaken. The Organisation has already suffered three years of under-budgeting. As a result, in 2003, just to keep up with the significant increase in the verification workload determined by yourselves, we will have to recruit 47 staff. To pay for this, the 2003 budget will have to be increased by more than 20 percent. This increase is simply non-negotiable. In full knowledge of this, major contributors have already made it clear that they will not agree to more than a 10 percent increase in 2003, which is not enough even to pay the salaries of existing staff. As a consequence, next year, regardless of the identity of the Director-

General, you will see a shrinking, not an expanding, Organisation for the Prohibition of Chemical Weapons, and an unavoidable reduction in its staff. And this will be the next step towards the Organisation's demise, because funding is being determined by political agendas, and, in a few capitals at least, the Organisation seems to be a very low priority.

Yes, there is too much at stake here – for the Organisation for the Prohibition of Chemical Weapons, for other international organisations, and for the international community. It is time to rise to the challenge. It is time to set priorities as they are perceived by all of you, and not just by a few so-called 'major players'. This is why I refused to resign under pressure from a small handful of Member States. I did so in order to give you all the opportunity to make your choice — to determine what future, if any, multilateral organisations have in this increasingly dangerous, complex, and unstable world.

You may be surprised to hear that, had I resigned and agreed to walk away, then my executioners would have granted me a 'dignified' departure, and that my accomplishments over five years of stewardship would even have been applauded. However, let me tell you: I do not need a hero's departure. But if I do go —something that is now in the hands of all of you – it will be with honour. I will have been faithful to the principles of integrity by which I have tried to live my professional and personal lives – principles which are shared by my family, my foreign service and my country's foreign policy. Please understand that, in refusing to resign, I chose the most arduous of the two paths. One that brought threats, risks, stress, and insecurity, but which I chose to follow. First of all, because that is the call of my conscience. Secondly, because the bulk of my 36 years in the Foreign Service have been devoted to the elaboration and strengthening of multilateral instruments, without which, I firmly believe, peace and harmony among nations will not be achieved. I therefore refuse to resign, *not* because I want to cling to my position; but because, in not resigning, I will be preserving the right of each one of you – of even the smallest Member State amongst you – to publicly state your position on this very serious issue and to conscientiously take responsibility for your decision. I consider it my duty to give you all, and not only the most powerful amongst you, the right to oust me.

Although this unprecedented, ruthless and arbitrary procedure is taking place away from the public limelight, beneath the low skies of the subdued city of The Hague, the decisions to be taken here over the next few days will leave an indelible mark on the history of international relations. I hope that all of you, the Member States, will confront this historic challenge in full awareness of the implications of your decision. The choices that you make during this session of the Conference will determine whether genuine multilateralism will survive, or whether it will be replaced by unilateralism in a multilateral disguise. The responsibility for this decision rests with you.

*   *   *   *

'Skirmish on Iraq Inspections'

Hans Blix is the Swedish diplomat who chairs the new United Nations team to inspect Iraq's weapons programmes. This report from the Washington Post (April 15, 2002) indicates that the purge of the international community may continue.

In an unusual move, Deputy Defence Secretary Paul D. Wolfowitz earlier this year asked the CIA to investigate the performance of Swedish diplomat Hans Blix, chairman of the new United Nations team that was formed to carry out inspections of Iraq's weapons programs. Wolfowitz's request, involving Blix's leadership of the International Atomic Energy Agency, illuminates the behind-the-scenes skirmishing in the Bush administration over the prospect of renewed United Nations weapons inspections in Iraq.

The government of Iraqi President Saddam Hussein is negotiating with UN Secretary General Kofi Annan on the return of arms inspectors, although Iraq asked Friday for a postponement of talks scheduled for next week. Iraq's UN ambassador said Baghdad did not want to divert attention from the Israeli-Palestinian crisis. Hussein has given no indication about whether he will agree to new inspections. But senior Pentagon civilians such as Wolfowitz and their allies elsewhere in the administration fear that a go-ahead by the Iraqi leader could delay and possibly fatally undermine their overall goal to launch a military campaign against Iraq.

The inspection issue has become 'a surrogate for a debate about whether we go after Saddam,' said Richard N. Perle, an adviser to Defense Secretary Donald H. Rumsfeld as chairman of the Defense Policy Board. Officials gave contradictory accounts of Wolfowitz's reaction to the CIA report, which the agency returned in late January with the conclusion that Blix had conducted inspections of Iraq's declared nuclear power plants 'fully within the parameters he could operate' as chief of the Vienna-based agency between 1981 and 1997.

A former State Department official familiar with the report said Wolfowitz 'hit the ceiling' because it failed to provide sufficient ammunition to undermine Blix and, by association, the new UN weapons inspection program. But an administration official said Wolfowitz 'did not angrily respond' when he read the report because he ultimately concluded that the CIA had given only a 'lukewarm assessment.' The official said the CIA played down US criticism of Blix in 1997 for closing the energy agency's books on Iraq after an earlier UN inspection program discovered Baghdad had an ongoing weapons development program.

Whatever the outcome, the request for a CIA investigation underscored the degree of concern by Wolfowitz and his civilian colleagues in the Pentagon that new inspections – or protracted negotiations over them – could torpedo their plans for military action to remove Hussein from power. 'The hawks' nightmare is that inspectors will be admitted, will not be terribly vigorous and not find anything,' said a former US official. 'Economic sanctions would be eased, and the US will be unable to act.'

A former member of the previous UN inspection team said the Wolfowitz group is 'afraid Saddam will draw us in to a diplomatic minuet.' ' While we will have disputes, they will be solved at the last minute and the closer it comes to the 2004 elections the more difficult it will be to take the military route,' the former official said.

Secretary of State Colin L. Powell and his associates at the State Department, who have been more cautious about a military campaign against Iraq, take a different view. They 'see the inspection issue as a play that buys time to enlarge a coalition for an eventual move against Saddam,' according to a former White House foreign policy specialist. State Department officials also argue that Hussein will inevitably create conditions for the failure of the UN inspections, by setting down unacceptable terms or thwarting the inspectors inside Iraq so they have to withdraw.

Blix's inspection organization – the UN Monitoring, Verification and Inspection Commission – has inherited the mandate from the UN Special Commission on Iraq, or UNSCOM. UNSCOM was established after the 1991 Persian Gulf War to eradicate all of Iraq's proscribed weapons before UN sanctions against Baghdad could be lifted. It was disbanded eight years later after the inspectors were withdrawn. In the event Iraq agrees to allow inspectors back, Blix and his associates have been establishing the framework for a new inspections program. In its resolution establishing the new commission, the UN Security Council offered to suspend sanctions on Iraq if it cooperates with the inspectors. 'The expression of full compliance is not used in the resolution,' noted Rolf Ekeus, the former executive chairman of UNSCOM. 'It states there shall be cooperation in all respects.'

Determining the level of cooperation required will be done by Blix based on a list of 'key remaining disarmament tasks,' according to the resolution. Among those tasks will be seeking to determine whether Iraq is continuing to develop the VX nerve agent, whether it has continued its medium- and long-range missile program, and searching for documents that could provide insight into Iraq's efforts to develop chemical and biological warheads.

Even if cooperation by Iraq led to suspending some sanctions, Baghdad would still be subject to UN monitoring of its weapons programs. Sanctions would not be formally lifted until it persuaded the Security Council, where the United States has veto power, that it had fully complied with its obligation to abandon its prohibited weapons programs.

In interviews, Blix said he will not use any of the most controversial methods, including eavesdropping, that UNSCOM employed to thwart Iraqi efforts to hide its weapons. His inspectors have all received 'cultural sensitivity' courses to avoid offending people, he said, but he insisted that he will give Iraq no 'discounts.' 'We do not see as our mandate to humiliate, harass or provoke,' Blix said.

The Bush administration is seeking to persuade Blix to scrap arrangements established by UNSCOM to govern inspections of sensitive sites. Ekeus, and his successor, Richard Butler, agreed to a set of procedures to govern inspection of sensitive sites that Iraq maintained were essential to its national security. A senior

U.S. official said he does not believe Blix intends to allow himself to 'be jerked around' by the Iraqis but that his inspection procedures are not yet 'ready for prime time.' 'Our basic position it that we will follow the practices of UNSCOM where we think they are purposeful and do not have negative consequences,' Blix said. 'We feel free to modify them if we do not think they are useful or are problematic.'

But Blix said he is obliged to honour a 1998 agreement between Annan and Iraq. It envisions a series of time-consuming procedures that would likely delay UN arms inspectors for about a week before they could gain access to more than 1,000 buildings contained in eight presidential sites. The procedures require that the inspectors provide Iraq with prior notification of an inspection, fly in a team of inspectors and senior diplomats and then hold a meeting with the foreign ministry. Blix said that if Iraq cooperates, he is confident that he could issue a report that would trigger a suspension of sanctions within a year after arriving in Baghdad.

© 2002 The Washington Post Company

EFFECTIVE
public services
NOT
open market
DOGMA

COMMUNICATION WORKERS UNION

If you'd like to help keep public services public, contact us on 020 8971 7200, fax us on 020 8971 7300, visit our web site at www.cwu.org or write to General Secretary Billy Hayes or President Andy Kerr at 150 The Broadway, Wimbledon, London, SW19 IRX.

THE BERTRAND RUSSELL PEACE FOUNDATION

PEACE DOSSIER

2002   Number 5

CRIMES IN PALESTINE

Mohammed Barakeh, Member of the Knesset, appealed to the International Court of Justice in a letter posted in Jerusalem on 9 April 2002. Israel's war on the Palestinians of the West Bank was then into its twelfth day.

'In the last ten days the whole world witnessed the state of Israel waging an all-out war against the civilian non-combatant Palestinian population in the West Bank. The Israeli Defence Forces, under orders from Ariel Sharon, the Israeli Prime Minister, General Shaul Mufaz, the Chief of Staff, and Benjamin Ben-Eliezer, the Minister of Defence, have committed atrocities in Ramallah, Bethlehem, Nablus, Jenin, Tulkarem, and every town and refugee camp they entered.

Under the pretext of "destroying the infrastructure of terrorism", the Israeli army is wreaking untold damage and sowing death in the towns it is re-occupying. The Israeli army has been arbitrarily shelling refugee camps, using helicopters, fighter jets, tanks and heavy artillery. This has caused the death of hundreds of people. Medical supplies are halted, hospitals raided, medical crews attacked, fired on or even used as human shields. Forms of collective punishment include starving the population, confining them to their homes under curfew, and destroying water pipes and electricity cables. The water supply to Ramallah has been shut off, endangering the lives of 120,000 Palestinians.

Most recently, there are reports that Israeli forces have committed a massacre in Jenin refugee camp. A war crime is being committed in Jenin. Jenin refugee camp has been pounded for the last four days by tanks, heavy artillery and fighter jets. More than one hundred civilians died. It is reported that hospitals have not received any bodies or injured persons. Corpses are left lying on the ground in the alleyways of Jenin, while the injured are bleeding to death. The refugee camp has run out of all supplies – water, food, and medical supplies.

Stop this massacre. The Palestinians being massacred need your help.

These atrocities constitute a war crime. They are a grave violation of international human rights law and humanitarian law. The state of Israel is throwing international law to the wall and crushing every single item of the Fourth Geneva Convention under its tanks.

The Israeli Prime Minister, Ariel Sharon, should stand before the international community to answer for the war crimes he has ordered. To this end, we call upon the International Court of Justice to send forthwith a fact-finding mission to the West Bank to document the crimes being committed; to gather evidence; and to hear testimonies and evidence by the Palestinians in the re-occupied towns. If this is impracticable at the moment due to the war launched by the Israeli army, we call upon the Court to send a fact-finding mission to areas from which the Israeli Defence Forces have withdrawn.

The international community should live up to its obligations. The inaction of the international organisations towards such blatant crimes is discrediting the force and essence of international law.'

SOLIDARITY WITH THE PALESTINIAN PEOPLE

The Russell Foundation sent a message to the International Conference of Solidarity with the Palestinian People which took place in Nicosia on 5/6 April 2002. It said:

The terrible assault by Israel on the people of Palestine, and the brutal military occupation of Ramallah, Bethlehem, Nablus, Jenin and other West Bank towns one after another, challenges peace movements everywhere and calls for a sustained and united response. The Israeli recourse to war is only one aspect of a runaway belligerence, with renewed and unrestrained American threats against Iraq, with a calculated rebuff to the peace initiative of the Arab Summit, and with the decision to respond to other humanitarian peace initiatives in the most humiliating, callous and intimidatory way.

In the face of war, and imminent threats of war, the peace movements need to generate powerful new pressures for peace, uniting the largest possible responses, not only in the region, but also throughout Europe and in the United Kingdom.

The just call for independent action by European states is widely supported, but it is being neutralised and blocked by the insistence that all joint state action must also involve the United States of America. But the United States is an active accomplice in the present bloody confrontations, and while all of us are in strong solidarity with American peace movements, and strongly support their protests in Washington on April 20th, we are bound, like many of them, to identify American military policy as the greatest threat to the entire region of the Middle East. In Britain, in particular, we need to call for independent initiatives to oppose all complicity in American military plans, while in the rest of the European Union we should support initiatives to promote peace and independent action alongside the other states in the region.

We welcome the initiative taken by AKEL to encourage joint action in this direction. We are aware of many other initiatives, including the attempts of the European Network for Peace and Human Rights to encourage the Cordoba dialogue between movements in Europe and the Middle East: but while these initiatives, and those concerned with the specific question of Palestine, will certainly continue, the present crisis is so severe, and its effects are likely to be so traumatising, that immediate action is called for, whatever other longer term steps may be taken later.

We believe that the peace movements should press a united call for: an immediate stop to the Israeli onslaught on the Palestinian people; permanent withdrawal of Israeli troops from Palestinian territories; an end to the siege of President Arafat and protection for his wellbeing; new initiatives to establish a Palestinian state, upholding 'the Palestinian people's inalienable right to self-determination and independent statehood', in the words of the final communiqué of the founding conference of the European Network for Peace and Human Rights.

FOR A WORLD WITHOUT NUCEAR WEAPONS

The 2002 World Conference against Atomic and Hydrogen Bombs takes place in the Japanese cities of Hiroshima and Nagasaki from 2nd to 9th August. The organisers have issued this call for support. More information is available on their web site (www.twics.com/~antiatom/).

Now, as the achievement of a peaceful 21st century is bearing more and more urgency for peoples across the world, there is a growing call for, and commitment to, the abolition of nuclear weapons. To contribute to developing the call into a truly global demand, and to open a window for a new era without nuclear weapons, we will hold the 2002 World Conference against Atomic and Hydrogen Bombs from August 2nd to 9th in Hiroshima and Nagasaki. The theme is, 'Working Together for a Peaceful and Promising World Without Nuclear Weapons'.

We call on all people in Japan and throughout the world who share the desire to build a world free of nuclear weapons to gather with the *Hibakusha* of Hiroshima and Nagasaki and with the victims of nuclear weapons from around the world to share ideas and actions and discuss agendas for a stronger anti-nuclear weapon movement. Last year, the governments of some non-nuclear weapon states which are striving for the abolition of nuclear weapons sent representatives to the Conference. The Conference was thus successful in establishing relations with governments and non-governmental organisations in support of the cause. We call on non-governmental organisations and local and national governments which support the abolition of nuclear weapons to participate in the Conference, either as representatives or individuals, regardless of social position, thought, belief or nationality.

As the voices in support of the abolition of nuclear weapons gained force, in 2000, 187 countries, including the 5 nuclear weapons states, reached agreement on an 'unequivocal undertaking to accomplish the total elimination of nuclear weapons'. This was epoch-making progress.

There has not been, however, any apparent initiative to make good on the undertaking. The largest nuclear weapons state, the United States, has gone so far as to make a policy on the actual use of nuclear weapons. The United States' development of 'usable' mini-nukes, its plan to resume underground nuclear test explosions in violation of the Comprehensive Test Ban Treaty, to which it had itself agreed, and its repeated sub-critical nuclear testing have all generated fear and concern across the globe. On the premise that it is fighting a 'war against terrorism', the United States has labelled certain countries as constituting an 'axis of evil' and laid out policies on waging war as it wishes. These actions are the exact opposite of what is required in order to eradicate terrorism and to build a peaceful world order. As a consequence there has been sharp criticism in Europe and Asia of United States 'unilateralism'.

We are also increasingly concerned about the future of our own country. The Japanese government's unquestioning subordination to the menacing, militaristic policies of the United States on issues such as the abolition of nuclear weapons and the nuclear test ban is extraordinary in the world. Given the presence of more than 100 United States military installations in Japan, there is a danger of the possible introduction of nuclear weapons into the country, in the violation of the Three Non-Nuclear Policies. There is even a danger of Japan being fully incorporated into a United States war. It is not military measures such as these, but true contribution to and initiatives for world peace that a majority of the Japanese people expect from their government.

In the 20th century, many people across the world joined forces to build what is now a strong current towards the abolition of nuclear weapons and a peaceful world order based on the United Nations Charter. Let us renew our commitment to the cause and reach out for ever wider co-operation in order to make this current sufficiently robust to overcome the challenges that confront it. We call on you to organise a drive for signatures and other creative actions of your own, and to support and take part in the nation-wide Peace March against Atomic and Hydrogen Bombs which will proceed to Hiroshima and Nagasaki from across Japan.

It is our sincere hope that people in Japan and throughout the world will join forces to build a wider and stronger movement, and that they will co-operate to achieve the cause of abolishing nuclear weapons. To this end we request your support and participation in the 2002 World Conference against Atomic & Hydrogen Bombs.

PEACE MOVEMENT GROWS IN UNITED STATES

Protest against the war at home and abroad took place across the United States during the weekend of 19-21 April. The Russell Foundation sent this message of support to the national demonstration in Washington which attracted over one hundred thousand people.

The war on terrorism has already spread into one country after another. The fighting draws in Afghanistan, Somalia, Yemen, the Philippines, Georgia, and who knows where next? Logically, it is quite impossible to know which countries might qualify as targets from one month to the next. Vast new military bases are spread out all across Central Asia, and the troop deployments that will be needed to staff them will involve whole armies. This is a war in search of enemies, and it will surely find them as its scope becomes more and more irrational.

We and other Europeans have for some time been worried about the military idea of full spectrum dominance, which, if it were not so threatening, would betoken megalomania.

Dominance, full spectrum or otherwise, is a guarantee of insecurity. To win security we need full spectrum democracy.

News of your plans for April 20 were brought to us by American friends who helped us found the European Network for Peace and Human Rights at the beginning of February. As a result of that meeting, Europeans have arranged supporting actions for this weekend in Belgium, Britain, Denmark, Greece, Holland and Sweden.

The European Network also agreed as a matter of priority to 'open a dialogue with the many movements in the United States working for peace and seek an exchange of delegations'.

We very much look forward to developing that dialogue and co-operation with yourselves .

US MILITARY WANTS SPACE-BASED BOMBER

Putting weapons in space is outlawed under the Outer Space Treaty. But that may not stop the United States: John Diedrich filed this story in the Gazette, Colorado Springs, in April 2002.

The military is looking into building a spacecraft that could drop bombs from space, fix orbiting satellites and give better pictures of the battlefield, the top space officer said Tuesday.

If a military space plane becomes a reality, it would be the first time theUnited States has put weapons in space. The Pentagon has military satellites that provide navigation, communication, weather, reconnaissance and missile warning information, all considered key to how the United States fights war. But none of them has weapons.

Gen. Ed Eberhart, head of US Space Command, Air Force Space Command and NORAD – all based in Colorado Springs – says the military needs a space plane. 'A reusable launch vehicle will be the key to operating and conquering the space frontier,' Eberhart said at the 18th annual National Space Symposium at The Broadmoor hotel, an annual exposition of commercial, military and civilian space issues. About 3,800 people attended.

NASA scrapped plans to build a spacecraft called the X-33 a year ago, in part, because of cost overruns. Eberhart said the military is interested in that spacecraft, but its version would be different. It might be designed to run without humans on board and to land in the oceans, he said.

A military space plane quickly could provide surveillance in areas of the world that become important to the Pentagon, he said. Moving satellites for better surveillance now can take days. It could fix or refuel satellites in orbit, which isn't a current option for the military. The plane also could bomb a target in a matter of hours, instead of the 17 hours it takes for a conventional bomber to travel halfway around the world. '(A space plane) has a lot of possibilities, a lot of applications in every one of our missions,' Eberhart said.

The space plane is only an idea and studying it doesn't mean the United States has decided to put weapons in space, said Army Maj. Barry Venable, spokesman for U.S. Space Command. 'We aren't doing our job if we don't look at things like this and think about it,' he said. Some critics of Space Command have said a space plane that drops bombs would be in violation of the 1967 Outer Space Treaty, which says 'space will be used for peaceful purposes.' But Venable said 'peaceful purposes' has been interpreted to mean nonaggressive acts. In other words, weapons can be put in space to defend a nation and its assets, he said.

Also Tuesday, Eberhart said information from military satellites may be useful for local police and other first responders in the war on terrorism. 'Over time we can leverage our space assets to support homeland security and law enforcement,' Eberhart said, noting there is no such proposal yet. 'A lot of it hinges on cooperation.' The general didn't give examples, but Venable said later satellite information could help fire departments track the spread of chemical or biological agents released by terrorists, provide police with more accurate city maps or give emergency workers better communications.

HOON 'WILLING TO USE' NUCLEAR WEAPONS

The World Court Project (www.gn.apc.org/wcp), an international citizens' network seeking implementation of the International Court's 1996 judgment on the illegality of nuclear weapons, prepared this briefing.

On 20 March 2002, Geoff Hoon, Secretary of State for Defence, appeared before the House of Commons Defence Select Committee. The subject was missile defence, but the evidence contains disturbing material on Britain's nuclear deterrence posture. The proceedings make it clear that the United Kingdom is prepared to use nuclear weapons against 'rogue' states or 'states of concern' such as Iraq if they use weapons of mass destruction – biological or chemical – not against the British homeland, but against troops in the field. The crucial disclosures start in paragraph 234 with a discussion about the United Kingdom's general deterrence in relation to a attack on the mainland. However, paragraph 236 moves on to a specific question from Jim Knight MP: *'Do you think such a state ['a state of concern'] would be deterred by our deterrent from using weapons of mass destruction against our forces in the field?'*

Mr Hoon's answer is *'... the United Kingdom possesses nuclear weapons and has the willingness and ability to use them in appropriate circumstances'*. In para 237 he says that *'... in the right conditions we would be willing to use our nuclear weapons ...'*. The context makes it quite clear that Mr Hoon is referring to a nuclear response by the United Kingdom to an attack using weapons of mass destruction on British troops in the field.

On 8 July 1996, the International Court of Justice (ICJ) confirmed that to threaten, let alone use, nuclear weapons would be generally contrary to International Humanitarian Law. The judges were unable to pronounce on whether they could be lawful *'in an extreme circumstance of self-defence, in which the very survival of a state would be at stake'*. Even then, any such threat or use should never violate the law. A typical letter from the Ministry of Defence to the World Court Project UK dated 15 December 1999 states that *'the United Kingdom would only consider using nuclear weapons in self-defence and in extreme circumstances, and subject to the rules of international law, and humanitarian law, applicable in armed conflict'*. This reflects faithfully the language of the ICJ. Many other letters and statements in Parliament are couched in similar terms.

Mr Hoon's evidence to the Select Committee flies directly in the face of such undertakings. A chemical or biological attack in the field could, by no stretch of the imagination, qualify as a threat to the survival of the British state. Whether such a response could ever be 'subject to the rules of international law, and humanitarian law, applicable in armed conflict' is also at issue in Mr Hoon's evidence. He says: *'we cannot rule out the possibility that such states [Iraq for example] would be willing to sacrifice their own people in order to make that kind of gesture [willingness to use Weapons of Mass Destruction]'*. If 'such states' were to 'sacrifice their own people', the agents of the sacrifice would be nuclear warheads launched by British Trident submarines. Saddam Hussein might be complicit in the sacrifice of innocent civilians; but it would be we who would be inflicting the sacrifice directly. This would almost certainly violate the need for the discriminate use of weapons demanded by International Humanitarian Law.

When the Committee next meets the Minister it should also ask him how a nuclear response by the United Kingdom on Iraq:
- could possibly be proportionate and discriminate,
- qualify as defending 'the very survival' of the British state,
- comply with the negative security assurances the United Kingdom has given all non-nuclear states,
- could avoid constituting a war crime.

*   *   *   *

On 29 April 2002, these issues were again pursued with Mr Hoon in the House of Commons in the following terms.

Mr. Malcolm Savidge (Aberdeen, North): Do the Secretary of State's recent comments concerning the possible use of nuclear weapons against Iraq signal a change of Government policy, whereby Britain is reneging on assurances given to non-nuclear weapons states under the nuclear non-proliferation treaty? Indeed, are the Government abandoning the policy of successive British Governments of regarding nuclear weapons as a deterrent of last resort?

Mr. Hoon: There has been no change in the British Government's policy – the use of nuclear weapons is still a deterrent of last resort. However, for that to be a deterrent, a British Government must be able to express their view that, ultimately and in conditions of extreme self-defence, nuclear weapons would have to be used.

PENNY ON TAX TO PAY FOR WAR ON AFGHANISTAN

Henry McCubbin comments on the Budget statement in Britain.

The Chancellor of the Exchequer, Gordon Brown, presented his Budget in April 2002. Much play was made of putting up tax to pay for more spending on the National Health Service. National Insurance contributions on almost all incomes are to rise by one per cent from April 2003. At the same time, personal allowances for tax-free pay are to be frozen, instead of up-rated with inflation, as is usual. This will mean all income taxpayers will pay more, and some low paid people will be taxed for the first time. The public justification for these tax and national insurance increases was writ large in the end of the Chancellor's speech. It was to improve the health of the nation. In fact, another £1 billion is to be found for the National Health Service this year.

Was that all that had to be paid for? Not at all. Tucked away between 'keeping to our fiscal rules' and 'an extra £125 million for foreign aid' was another large item of expenditure. A extra £1 billion had to be found this year for spending on defence which had already been incurred. The Chancellor said:

'Since September 11th we have made provision of 50 million pounds for our domestic security responsibilities and, over the last year, 950 million pounds for defence. We will continue to meet our responsibilities internationally and to our armed forces'.

Out of a total of 9,131 words in his speech, Gordon Brown devoted 2,221 to the NHS and just 39 to the extra billion pounds for military spending. That's what I call spin.

Reviews

Bombing

Sven Lindqvist, *A History of Bombing*, Granta, 2002, 399 sections, £7.99, ISBN 1 86207 490 9

The Swedish writer, Sven Lindqvist, is one of the most challenging and original voices on the European left, with over twenty five books to his credit, covering a vast scope that includes political economy, travelogue, history, autobiography and literary criticism. Erudite, allusive and genre-breaking, his work combines exhaustive scholarly research with a mordant wit and an uncompromising determination to confront unpleasant truths about Europe's historical relationship with the Third World.

Despite his own impressive academic record, Lindqvist has always been wary of the tendency within academia to dehumanise and objectify the subjects of its research and render its findings inaccessible through the use of dry academic jargon. In the introduction to *Land and Power in Latin America* (1979), a typically idiosyncratic personal investigation into the political economy of Latin America, Lindqvist wrote of academic texts on the same subject that 'In these books no one utters a word – one never sees a living face, nor a landscape. The soil has no smell. The screams are never heard'.

The same cannot be said of Lindqvist's own work, in which the victims of history can be heard and seen, and the crimes committed against them are painstakingly revealed. His books are all characterised by the same moral passion and humanistic concern, the same refusal to accept the established rules of academic discourse, the same search for a new way of writing about history and politics.

A major thread running through his work is the historical impact of imperialism and its racist underpinnings in European thought. In an era in which the history of imperialism is being re-written to justify new and equally insidious forms of conquest, Lindqvist's work represents a sustained and irrefutable indictment of the historical crimes that have been expunged from the official record. In *Exterminate the Brutes* (1995), an anonymous traveller who may or may not be Lindqvist himself, journeys across Africa, using the words from Conrad's deranged Colonel Kurtz as the basis for a journey into the European heart of darkness and an exploration of the genocidal impulse in European civilisation, from the colonial battlegrounds of Omdurman and the Belgian Congo to the Nazi holocaust. *Desert Divers* (2000) continued that journey, in an evocative deconstruction of the way that the romantic European colonial imagination invented the Sahara Desert during the nineteenth century, alternating essays and historical vignettes on famous European travellers to North Africa, with the meditations of Lindqvist's enigmatic narrator.

A History of Bombing takes these investigations further, and remains as provocative and unclassifiable as its predecessors. It is written in 399 short pieces, none of them more than half a page long, connected thematically by arrows and numbers to construct a kind of narrative maze with no obvious beginning or end. Each section is a self-contained piece, ranging from autobiographical anecdotes about Lindqvist's own boyhood discovery of aerial bombing on the eve of World War Two, to descriptions of early uses of strategic bombing by the Italians in Libya, the Spanish in Morocco, and the bombing of Hiroshima, Korea and Vietnam. Lindqvist has constructed his book so that the reader can 'enter' the text at various suggested points, tracing different narrative sequences back and forth according to different themes, or simply at their own whim.

The experience is initially confusing and disorientating. Put the book down in the morning and you will not remember where you were the night before or how you got there, without having to retrace your steps. But this is not just a tricksy literary device. In the introduction, Lindqvist declares that this is no ordinary book, and his deliberate subversion of the conventions of linear narrative is perfectly suited to the tangential way his mind and imagination works, in which connections are made between events, ideas and people that may not seem obvious, or uncovering facts that other historians have either ignored or considered unimportant.

One of the most striking and original features of the book is the way that Lindqvist draws on obscure literary sources, as well as historical facts, weaving in extracts from long-forgotten Edwardian science fiction novels to the apocalyptic Nazi ravings of The Turner Diaries alongside the historical crimes he describes. In the process he exposes a terrifying continuum in European thinking far removed from the liberal humane model that many Europeans would like to believe is the essence of their civilisation. Here is Desmond Shaw in the 1926 novel *Ragganok*, describing the future use of the British Air Force to defend London against invasion by African soldiers 'with their white eyes rolling in their black faces':

'The British planes ... simply sprayed into and over the black wretches, who began at once to rush about screaming as their bodies took fire ... in vain did they try to escape from the incinerating fire which just ... left the stench of charred flesh ... in vain did they fling themselves into the Thames, already full of the bodies of their victims.'

This gallant act of extermination saves the day, thanks to our magnificent men in their flying machines, but, as Lindqvist points out, these fantasies of racial domination and technological dominance were already being played out for real in the colonies, as an internal British military report on the impact of aerial bombing to suppress a colonial revolt in 1924 makes clear.

'Where the Arab and Kurd had just begun to realise that if they could stand a little noise, they could stand bombing... they now know what real bombing means, in casualties and damage: they now know that within forty-five minutes a full-sized village can be practically wiped out and a third of its inhabitants killed or injured by four or five machines which offer them no real target, no opportunity for glory as warriors, no effective means of escape'.

That report was written by Arthur 'Bomber' Harris, the architect of strategic bombing whose bombs would later rain down on the civilian populations of

Hamburg, Dresden and Berlin. Harris first developed his lifelong fascination with strategic bombing during the 2nd Afghanistan war in 1908, and the meticulous and sardonic revelation of his grim career trajectory is typical of Linqvist's method. Whether he is discussing the fraudulent pretensions of 'surgical precision' bombing or analysing the spurious justification for bombing Hiroshima and Nagasaki, Lindqvist is a relentless and uncompromising investigator and a writer in total control of his material. The result is a book so dense and rich in its remorseless accumulation of anecdotes and historical detail, that the reader leaves it exhausted, right up to its final grim pronouncement:

> 'Throughout this century, it has been clear that the standard of living enjoyed by the industrialised countries cannot be extended to the world's population. We have created a way of life that must always be limited to a few. Those few can make up a broad middle class in some countries, and a narrow upper class in the rest. The members know each other by their buying power. They have a common interest in preserving their privileges, by force if necessary. They, too, are born into violence. Out of this violence, both that which has already been committed and that which is still dormant, the century's dreams of dominance emerge. The injustice we defend forces us to hold on to genocidal weapons, with which our fantasies can be realised whenever we like. Global violence is the hard core of our existence. And that which is yet to come.'

A History of Bombing was written before September 11th, but recent events have borne out Lindqvist's predictions only too accurately. Once again our politicians and generals are leading us into war against the barbarians, and the Pentagon's megalomaniac fantasies of 'Full Spectrum Dominance' have been carefully subsumed within the war against terrorism in order to make them more palatable to the public. Now when so many Western intellectuals have swallowed the American-led crusade without criticism, when bombs are still falling on Afghanistan and more may shortly be falling on Iraq in the name of freedom and human rights, this book is a salutory corrective to liberal self-delusion, and we should be grateful for Lindqvist's single-minded trawl through the dark sewers of our recent history.

Matt Carr

Islam and September 11

Tariq Ali, *The Clash of Fundamentalisms*, Verso, £15 hardback, ISBN 1 85984 679 3

Tariq Ali is well-known as a left-wing political activist, broadcaster, journal editor and novelist, in Britain and more widely in the English speaking world, which includes the Indian sub-continent. In his latest book, *The Clash of Fundamentalisms*, Tariq has set out to help us to understand the background to the attacks on the World Trade Centre and the Pentagon on September 11, 2001. This involves him in giving us a potted history of Islam, a long exposition of the origins of the Arab-Israeli conflict, and a detailed examination of the dialectical development of the two fundamentalisms, which are referred to in the book's title – that of the Islamic Wahhabi and of United States born-again Christians. He is able to do this from the position of a 'non-Moslem Moslem', whose family were well-connected Punjabi landowners who found themselves on the Pakistan side of the border at the partition of the Indian Empire in 1947. In that year Tariq was not quite four years old and from then on he rejected all religious instruction. After studying at Oxford University he stayed in England while making frequent trips to Pakistan, whenever he was permitted to do so. The book is greatly enriched by Tariq's personal reminiscences.

Islam's Strengths and Weaknesses

The history of Islam, and equally of the Arabs, is one concerning which most Europeans are profoundly ignorant. The reason is the same as in the case of African history, though with much less justification, to wit, that colonial rulers did not wish to recognise that the peoples they had conquered and even enslaved had any history. It was conveniently forgotten that by 800 AD the influence of Islam had spread west to the Atlantic in Portugal and east to the Hindu Kush. Baghdad, the capital of the Abbasid empire, had by then a population of two million. It is an essential part of Tariq's story to demonstrate the debt which civilisation owes to the Arab Islamic scholars for preserving the knowledge of the classical world and developing the mathematical studies of the East. Tourists who visit Spain are able to appreciate the riches of Moorish architecture, but few realise that at a time when Oxford or Cambridge libraries in the 13th Century contained a few hundred books, the library of Cordoba held 400,000.

The Ottoman Empire of the Turks, which added the Balkans to Islamic influence has gained a particularly unedifying reputation, still worse that of the Mongols who added Central Asia and India. But the tourist who visits Istanbul or Cairo or Delhi or Samarkand will know of the beauty of the Mughal buildings. In his 1930s travelogue *The Road to Oxiana*, Robert Byron described the wonders of Islamic art in what is now Afghanistan, but it is unlikely that anything will be left of it after American carpet bombing.

The question inevitably arises in the reader's mind as to how it was that Islam collapsed first in face of Christian conquest in 15th Century Spain and again in face of British, French and Russian conquests in the 18th and 19th. Centuries. There were divisions between the three Caliphates – Cordoba, Cairo and Baghdad, and divisions in Islam between Sunnis and Shiites and, after the 1740s, the Wahhabis. The successive Islamic empires were immensely extended and based upon trade routes which could be, and were, interrupted. Before it yielded to the Reyes Catolicos in 1492, Cordoba was riddled with heresies. A great part of its attraction, as Tariq comments, were 'the joys of heresy'. The Spanish Christians developed a confidence and military organisation as they marched over many years southwards through Spain to oust the Moors, a confidence that carried them successfully into the Americas against peoples who had no metal armour and no horses. Part of that confidence came from their belief in a divine will, but Islam shared the same mono-theism. There must have been something in the fact that the Moors came originally from outside Spain, outside Europe.

The Ottomans and Mughals did not lack in confidence and military organisation and they did not suffer any more than the Europeans from internal divisions. What the Europeans had done by the 16th Century was to develop the technological basis for industrialisation through their ship building and capitalist agriculture. The British army had a self-confidence in their victories over the French, which in part enabled Clive to win the battle of Plassey in 1757, but this was really achieved by his winning over the support of Omichund the wealthy Hindu merchant of Calcutta. For where else except in trade with Britain could such merchant wealth be sustained? The development in Britain of industry and especially of an arms industry had changed everything. But why had this not happened in the lands of Islam? India produced steel before Europe and cotton production for export in what is now Bangladesh, against which Lancashire's early cotton manufacturers demanded 100% protection by the British government, until their machines were more efficient than the Indian craftsmen.

The fact was that industrial production was first developed in Europe and especially in Britain and not elsewhere. Existing empires in China, India, Central Asia, Africa and the Americas fell before the advancing Europeans and, once brought into their colonial systems, their peoples were held back in their development and still suffer from the colonial experience. But why only in Europe? Tariq suggests that Islam never had a Reformation such as Christianity experienced in the 16th Century. Arabs and Muslim Indians suffered from this lack. Perhaps, that is to give too strong an influence to the Protestant ethic in the rise of capitalism. This ethic was very evident in Britain, the Netherlands and France and among the European settlers in America. But Russia and Japan and later China and Korea succeeded in industrialisation without a Protestant ethic.

There is another possible explanation for the decline of Islam, which is not entirely dissociated from the Reformation. The Reformation broke up Christian Europe and the Holy Roman Empire into nation states. Capitalism developed under the protection of the nation state. The unity of Islam was preserved despite differences between Shiites and Sunnis and Wahhabis. In particular there was no Arab state. Although there were many kingdoms, none had the authority of the European nation state, and the fact is that the European Powers did their best to ensure that none ever had that authority. The changes in Great Power support given to royal families in Turkey, Egypt, Afghanistan, (Trans)Jordan, Iraq, Iran, and Saudi Arabia, let alone in Greece and the Balkans, have moved like a kaleidoscope, but with the intention of the Powers always that none should be the same colour at the same time. From this we can easily deduce the tragedy of the Arabs in Palestine, caught between their desire for Arab unity and a Palestine state.

The Jewish-Arab Conflict

Contrary to widespread belief, the Jewish diaspora was not the result of Arab incursion into Palestine; it goes back to the Roman Empire. Tariq describes the final freeing of Jerusalem from the successive Christian crusades to liberate the holy (Christian) places from Islam in the following succinct paragraph, which deserves quotation in full:

'Saladin's long march finally ended in victory. Jerusalem was taken in 1187 and once again made an open city. The Jews were provided with state subsidies to rebuild their synagogues. The churches were left untouched. No revenge killings were permitted. Like Caliph Umar five hundred years before him, Saladin proclaimed the freedom of the city for worshippers of all faiths. But his failure to take Tyre was to prove a costly tactical error. Pope Urban despatched the Third Crusade to take back the Holy City and Tyre became their vital base of operations. Their leader Richard Plantagenet reoccupied Acre, executing prisoners and drowning its inhabitants in blood, but Jerusalem survived. It could not be retaken. For the next seven hundred years the city with the exception of one short-lived and inconsequential Crusader occupation, remained under Muslim rule. During this period no blood soiled its pavements.'

The seven hundred years (731 to be exact) takes us to 1918. 1917 was not only the year of the Russian Revolution but also of General Allenby's entry into Jerusalem after defeating the Turkish armies with the support of Lawrence's Saudi Arab friends. It was followed by the Balfour Declaration promising a 'national home for the Jews', made in exchange for continuing loans from New York to sustain Britain's war effort. The national home, it was said, should not affect the rights of the other inhabitants. So Palestine was annexed by Britain under what was later termed 'a mandate' from the League of Nations. Thus from the very start the Arab-Jewish conflict in Palestine was a compound of American money and British duplicity. In the 20 years from 1919 to 1939 about 300,000 Jews emigrated mainly from Germany to Palestine making a Jewish population of about 400,000, or somewhat less than half the number of Arabs and three times the number of Christians. The holocaust in Nazi Germany and anti-Semitism in Russia further increased the Jewish population after 1945.

European settlers overseas, whether in the Americas, Australia and New Zealand, Kenya or Southern Africa, have always spread the myth that they came to occupy an empty land. In truth they had done much to empty it by destroying the indigenous peoples. In all cases there was bitter resistance. The first Palestinian *intifada* was in 1936-9, and to crush it required the deployment of 25,000 British troops and Zionist auxiliaries helped by bomber squadrons of the RAF . The Zionists have spread the same myth of 'a land without people' about Palestine. But in the diaries of the founder of Zionism, which Tariq quotes , Herzl wrote in 1895.

'We shall try to spirit the penniless across the border by procuring employment for it in the transit countries, while denying it any employment in our country. Both the process of expropriation and the removal of the poor must be carried out discreetly and circumspectly.'

By 1938 the then Zionist leader Ben-Gurion was defending the concept of 'compulsory transfer' arguing that

'I favour partition of the country because when we become a strong power after the establishment of the [Israeli] state, we will abolish partition and spread throughout all of Palestine.'

In the event, expropriation was not carried out 'discreetly and circumspectly' but by open military actions – a million Arabs in the 1948 war into exile or refugee camps, and most of the rest into the occupied territories after the 1967 war, and finally by intimidation in the Gaza strip and the West Bank today.

Arab Disunity

The question remains why the neighbouring Arab states did not protect, and still have not protected, their fellow religionists. It took fifteen years for them even to recognise Yassir Arafat and the PLA (Palestine Liberation Army). The answer, Tariq says, lies under the ground. The Middle East has the largest reserves of oil in the world, and the largest untapped reserves lie around the Caspian Sea. These last could be accessed via Russia, Turkey or Afghanistan. Surprise, surprise! Both George Bush and his son George W. are Texan oil men. At one time, not so long ago, Texan oil companies had talks in Houston with the Taliban about an oil pipeline across Afghanistan. But for much longer than that the Middle East policies of Britain and then of the United States have been dominated by the need to control the rich oil supplies in the region, and this meant keeping the Russians out.

The United States has done all in its power – and it has a lot of power – to ensure that there are governments friendly to them throughout the region. This has not been without its difficulties, because it has involved not only supporting despotic rulers like President Musharraf of Pakistan, and earlier the Shah of Persia and the Saudis, as well as the aggressive Israelis. It also meant financing and arming those who are now the 'axis of evil' – despots like Saddam Hussein so that he should conduct an eight year war against revolutionary Iran and recruiting the 'terrorist' mujahadeen of Osama bin Laden so that they should fight against the Russians in Afghanistan. Only then to find that they turned against their erstwhile masters. Even today, it is announced that Arafat's police chief will be protected from Israeli troops, because he has, or had, links with the Central Intelligence Agency and Israeli security forces. Nothing is quite what it seems when a hegemonic power uses its secret service to advance its aims.

Turkish rule over the Middle Eastern countries throughout the Nineteenth Century was supported by Britain, France and Russia because none of these three wished either of the others or Germany to occupy the vacuum which would be created by Turkish collapse. In the meantime, each took some form of 'protection' over the several parts of the Ottoman Empire where their interests lay – the Russians in the Black Sea and Central Asia, the French in Syria and Algeria, the British in Egypt (with special reference to Suez, the route to India), Palestine and Persia (to control Anglo-Persian oil). The Germans in their *drang nach Osten* had their eye on Baghdad and on alliance with the Turks which they cemented in 1914. Finally the Americans, in 1933, by bribing the Saudi monarch won the concession to drill for oil in Saudi Arabia, where oil production began in 1938.

The Dialectic of the Two Fundamentalisms

The Russian Revolution in 1917 sent a shock wave through all the oppressed peoples in the Ottoman Empire and Austro-Hungarian Empire even more than in the French and British Empires, just because Russia was that much nearer. National liberation movements from the Turks had been everywhere stultified by Great Power intervention and even occupation, as by the British in Egypt. The result of the Revolution was to force these movements into extreme forms of resistance and terrorism. Communist Parties emerged in Egypt, Iran and Iraq as well as in the Indian Empire, but they found themselves in competition with long standing movements for Islamic revivalism inside the Ottoman Empire. From the middle of the Eighteenth Century Ibn Wahhab had been preaching an ultra-sectarian *jihad* against the deviations from the true Islamic faith. This was nothing new but he combined it with social prescriptions of punishment beatings, stoning of adulterers, hand and arm amputation of thieves, repression of women, and with a political alliance that was to determine the future of what the Europeans called the 'Middle East'.

This was the alliance through marriage of Wahhabi's daughter and the Saudi family. As Tariq writes:

'This combination of religious fanaticism, military ruthlessness, political villainy and the press-ganging of women to cement alliances was the foundation stone of the dynasty that rules Saudi Arabia today.'

Although the Saudi's wings were clipped in 1811 by Muhammed Ali's seizure of power in Egypt and his defeat of the Saud-Wahhabi forces in the Hijaz , the Saudis were able just over a century later, in alliance with the power of the British Empire to establish themselves once more as a regional power and later, as Tariq concludes,

'Another and even more powerful imperial state would entrust them with the entire [Arabian] peninsula. Wahhabism in its purest form – an unalloyed mixture of confessional rigidity and political opportunism – had become an instrument of the infidel.'

Tariq gives us this history because it is out of this combination of military ruthlessness and Islamic Puritanism, the latter seen by the fundamentalists of today to have been abandoned by the Saudis in their ostentatious wealth and finally in their concession of a military base to the Americans for the Gulf War, that Osama bin Laden drew his levy of Wahhabi Arabs to form, together with the Muslim Brotherhood of Egypt, the al-Quaida and the image of the true Islam in the Taliban of Afghanistan.

But for this to happen, Tariq tells us that we have to recognise, first, that the British Military Intelligence was in contact with the Muslim Brotherhood from its foundation as an anti-Communist armed underground in Egypt in 1928 and, second, that the United States secret services financed and supported Bin Laden, as their agent against the Soviet action in Afghanistan, just as they had supported Saddam Hussein in their machinations against Soviet influence in Iraq and then in Iran. Terrorism, the 'axis of evil' against which President Bush is now crusading, with British support, is thus the direct product of American and British world-wide subversive response to the Soviet challenge. That this did not stop at resistance to the emergence of Communist Parties but extended to all liberation movements can be seen from the Central Intelligence Agency inspired coups not only against the Communist Party in Indonesia but against Ben Bella in Algeria, Nkrumah in Ghana, Goulart in Brazil, as well as Kassem in Iraq and Mossadeq in Iran, while in Egypt the Muslim Brotherhood attempted three times to kill Nasser, a nationalist like the others on the CIA list and no Communist. Indeed, Tariq makes the point that the Soviet advice to Nasser on the eve of the 1967 Israeli-Egyptian war was not to provoke an Israeli attack, which left him quite unprepared for the attack when it came.

Tariq's concept of a 'clash of fundamentalisms' correctly describes the growth of fundamentalism among Islamic societies and equally of a somewhat similar fundamentalism in the moralistic claims that accompany the United States' assumption of world hegemony. Tariq is right that there is a dialectic at work here when he shows how each has encouraged the other. It is not envy or distaste at the wealth and technology of the United States, that inspires the suicide bombers, as Mr Bush would have Americans believe, but despair at ever getting out from under American surveillance and American repression of any and every act of self-liberation. The list of United States direct military interventions since 1945 – China, Korea, Guatemala (three times), Indonesia, Cuba, the Congo, Peru, Laos, Viet Nam, Cambodia, Grenada, Libya, El Salvador, Nicaragua, Panama, Iraq, Bosnia, Sudan, Yugoslavia, Afghanistan – still leaves out indirect intervention through provision of arms and financial support for local armed war lords like Mobutu and Savimbi in Africa and those which Tariq has been uncovering for us in the world of Islam, and which we can see for ourselves now in Israel.

This is not, however, a 'clash of civilisations' as writers like Samuel Huntington have proposed, and as President Bush suggests in his use of the word 'crusade' for what he envisages as the proper response to the events of September 11th. Civilisation is one human process, to which many peoples have contributed over the centuries and to which Islam, as Tariq has reminded us, has made a great contribution. The greatest damage to our common civilisation has come from the fomenting of violence, the encouragement of terrorists and it may still all be destroyed by a nuclear explosion more devastating than Hiroshima and Nagasaki, for which the United States must bear the ultimate responsibility. The danger of nuclear war today must be regarded as more serious than at any time since the worst moments of American-Soviet nuclear rivalry. What Tariq reveals as the response of fundamentalists in Pakistan and in India to the bombing of Afghanistan is frightening.

The kaleidoscope of changes in political allegiance is nowhere more clearly illustrated than in the case of Pakistan. As the main base for resistance to a 'socialist' India and to the election in western Pakistan of socialists like Zulfiqar Ali Bhutto and later his daughter Benazir, the top brass of the Pakistan Army was for long regarded by the United States as the training ground for their favourite military dictators. They were often raised to power or supported in power by appeal to Islamic fundamentalism. The Pakistan Inter Services Intelligence (ISI), according to Tariq the 'most powerful institution in the country', was, moreover, responsible for the training and arming of militants to join the *jihad* against the Soviet occupation of Afghanistan and in the aftermath of the Soviet withdrawal for establishing the Taliban in power. With the collapse of the Soviet Union and the end of the Cold War, Pakistan's generals fell from favour and when they exploded a nuclear advice they were cut off from US aid – until once again they were needed, after September 11th, this time to provide a base for United States action against the very forces in Afghanistan which they had earlier created.

Worse even than the Taliban are the fundamentalist forces which have been generated in Pakistan itself, and, given an almost equal growth of fundamentalism in India, Tariq sees that the danger grows of war escalating over Kashmir into a nuclear exchange. They that sow the wind are reaping the whirlwind. The actions in Afghanistan against the Soviet Union were paid for by encouraging the growing of poppies in that country and the heroin business has spread from there along with the Moslem fighters to Bosnia and Kosovo, Chechnya and the Philippines. Now the Christian fundamentalism which has emerged in America is encouraging the launching of a new war against Iraq, and Mr Bush and Mr Blair are having to cry 'Halt! enough is enough' to America's very own first ally, Israel, lest its military incursion into the Occupied Territories should embroil the whole region in bloodshed.

We desperately need in the West a new tolerance, space for peoples as well as nation states and recognition of the inequalities imposed by imperialism, if we are to match Tariq's appeal to the world of Islam for

'a rigid separation of state and mosque; the dissolution of the clergy; the assertion by Muslim intellectuals of their right to interpret the texts that are the collective property of Islamic culture as a whole; the freedom to think freely and rationally and the freedom of imagination.'

And we need to support action for peace with Milton's words to General Fairfax at the siege of Colchester in 1648, 'For what can war, but endless war still breed?'

Michael Barratt Brown

Letters to Socialists

Marx and Engels Collected Works, Volume 49, Frederick Engels Letters 1890-1892, Lawrence and Wishart, 640 pp. £45 hardback, ISBN 085315 625 5

This immense collaboration is moving towards its close. The final volume is to be expected next year, 2003, and with it we shall have all the known works of Marx and Engels, including all their correspondence and some newly discovered works.

Volume 49 consists of letters from Engels to a very wide cross-section of Socialist leaders around Europe. It begins in 1890 with a letter to Liebknecht, and it goes on until 1892, with a letter to Karl Kautsky. Seven hundred and eleven pages work through virtually all the problems of the contemporary Socialist movement, especially those associated with the development of the Second International.

Strongly represented are letters about the upsurge of the new unionism in Great Britain, and candid commentaries on the progress of this movement. Engels remained in close contact with William Thorne of the gas workers, whose Union established itself to become the rock upon which was built the present General Municipal and Boilermakers' Union. Ben Tillett and John Burns from the dockers were in regular contact with Engels.

All these letters come to us from a different age. One wonders when Engels ever found time to do anything else but write letters. And yet this correspondence is shot through with detailed advice, and betokens a most comprehensive knowledge of the state of play in all the different Socialist Parties it covers... and, of course, in between this epistolary labour, Engels was editing the final volume of Marx's *Capital* which involved him, as he said, in working through all the original documentation and argument of the book, in order to ensure the accuracy of the version which he was preparing for the press.

If it is true that Marxism has gone out of fashion, then it should be possible to acquire these mighty volumes for another day. Whatever happens to the fashion, they give us an extraordinary insight into their times.

More than half the letters featured here are newly translated, and have not appeared in English before.

KC

Contradictions

Leo Panitch and Colin Leys (editors), *Socialist Register 2002 : A World of Contradictions*, Merlin Press, pp.294, ISBN 0 85036 502 3 £30.00 hardback, ISBN 0 85036 501 5 £14.95 paperback

It was the central message of Marx's more deterministic prophesies that there were intrinsic contradictions in the very processes of industrial capital accumulation that would lead to the collapse of the system and create the working class that would supplant it with a socialist system. That capitalism has survived for 150 years since Marx first made his prophesy and appears indeed rather to have grown in strength, despite some ups and downs, and that a working class socialist succession seems as far away as ever, has for long been an embarrassment to all good comrades.

In the latest issue of the *Socialist Register*, the editors have invited a number of mainly Canadian Marxists to explore the present 'world of contradictions' to discover what may be learnt from them. Readers would be well advised to read first Ellen Meiksin Woods' final essay, which brilliantly explains 'contradictions' in capitalism in the sense, as she puts it, 'that the very forces that produce an irreducible systemic need at the same time constitute a barrier to the fulfilment of that need.'

The first essay sets the question for the whole volume. This is a thoughtful examination by Naomi Klein of the Porto Alegre process, in which she seeks to unravel the many threads that have been woven together in the anti-globalisation protests from Seattle onwards. If this is the 'Internet come to life', what form could it take, she asks, that could take protest into positive action for social change? Some elements of Marx's working class may be involved, but they are neither central to the process nor at all united in their perspective. Then, what? Unfortunately, the authors do not tell us.

What they do offer are a number of interesting essays on the various attempts made by the owners and controllers of global capital, and by the governments of leading capitalist states, most particularly the United States, to overcome or at least to regulate the most obvious contradictions. These have become much less susceptible of management in the age of so-called 'neo-liberalism', since the removal of the 'Soviet threat', and the consequent ending of the perceived need to accommodate working class aspirations.

None the less, we have to recognise the apparent success of United States economic recovery after the decline in 2001. Moreover, the operations of the G7 Financial Stability Reform and the G10 Central Bank Governors, together with the work of such bodies as the International Association of Insurance Supervisors and Basle Committee on Banking Regulations and Supervisory Practices do provide information and warnings and some form of regulation that did not exist in the 1930s.

In the long run, and it may indeed be very long, the two major contradictions must come to a head – in the increasing imbalance of the growth in productive capacity of accumulated capital compared with the restricted purchasing power of increasingly unequal incomes and the limited energy and physical capacities of the planet. What the result may be of the emergence of a single centre of economic power combined with overwhelming military and political power in the 'full spectrum dominance' of the United States is only hinted at by these authors. But their arguments must lead to the conclusion that, with no countervailing forces, the contradictions become only the more intractable.

MBB

From Kosovo to Kabul

*Human Rights and
International Intervention*
David Chandler
Preface by Edward S. Herman

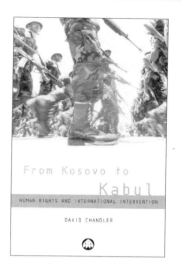

The UN and Nato's new policy of
interventionism – as shown in Bosnia,
Kosovo and East Timor – has been
hailed as 'humanitarian action'. David
Chandler reveals the worrying political
implications of this new human rights
discourse. He asks why the West can
prioritise the human rights of
individuals over the traditional rights of
state sovereignty and why this shift has
happened so quickly.

March 2002 • Pb • £14.99 • 0 7453 1883 5

Water Wars

Pollution, Profits and Privatization
Vandana Shiva

"The world's most prominent radical scientist." **The Guardian**

Vandana Shiva, a world-renowned environmentalist and
campaigner, examines the 'water wars' of the twenty-first century:
the aggressive privatization by the multinationals of communal water
rights. Shiva calls for a movement to preserve water access for all, and
offers a blueprint for global resistance based on examples of
successful campaigns.

March 2002 • Pb • £12.99 • 0 7453 1837 1

P L U T O **P R E S S**

Independent Progressive Publishing
www.plutobooks.com